The Only Living Trusts Estate Planning Guide

Protect Your Assets, Avoid Probate, Slash Taxes and Secure Your Heirs' Future.

Thayer Sterling

ISBN 979-8-89860-845-3

Table of Contents

Introduction

Living trusts are a vital tool in modern estate planning, offering numerous benefits that can help ensure your assets are managed and distributed according to your wishes. Unlike a will, which only takes effect after death and must go through the probate process, a living trust becomes effective immediately upon its creation and can be managed by you during your lifetime. This offers greater flexibility, privacy, and control over your estate. A living trust, also known as an intern Vivas trust, allows you to transfer ownership of your assets into a trust while you are still alive. This means that you, as the grantor, can continue to use and manage these assets, but they are legally owned by the trust. You appoint a trustee to manage the trust according to your instructions, and you can also name successor trustees to take over in the event of your incapacity or death.

There are several key advantages to creating a living trust:

Avoiding Probate: One of the most significant benefits of a living trust is that it helps avoid the probate process. Probate can be a lengthy and expensive procedure, and it is also a matter of public record. A living trust allows for the private and efficient transfer of assets to your beneficiaries without the need for court intervention. Managing Incapacity: A living trust provides a mechanism for managing your assets if you become incapacitated. If you are no longer able to handle your financial affairs, your designated successor trustee can step in and manage the trust assets on your behalf, ensuring that your finances remain in order and your wishes are followed Flexibility and Control: With a living trust, you retain control over your assets during your lifetime. You can amend or revoke the trust as your circumstances change, ensuring that your estate plan remains current and reflective of your wishes. Privacy: Unlike a will, which becomes a public document during the probate process, a living trust remains private. This means that the details of your estate and the distribution of your assets are not disclosed to the public. Potential Tax Benefits: While a living trust itself does not provide direct tax advantages, it can be part of a broader estate planning strategy that includes tax planning to minimize estate taxes and other liabilities. This book is designed to guide you through the entire process of creating and managing a living trust. We will cover everything from the initial steps of assessing your assets and choosing a trustee, to drafting the trust document, funding the trust, and maintaining it over time. You will also learn about the legal aspects of living trusts, how to avoid common mistakes, and how to ensure that your trust is up-to-date and compliant with current laws. By the end of this book, you will have a thorough understanding of living trusts and the confidence to create and manage one effectively, ensuring that your estate is protected, and your wishes are honoured. Whether you are just beginning to consider your estate planning options or looking to refine and update your existing plans, this book will serve as a valuable resource to help you achieve your goals.

Chapter 1: Initial Steps in Creating a Living Trust

Creating a living trust is a significant step in estate planning, one that requires careful consideration and meticulous planning. The process begins with a comprehensive assessment of your assets, which forms the foundation of your living trust. Knowing what you own, understanding the value of your assets, and documenting them properly are crucial first steps in this journey.

Assessing Your Assets

The first task in creating a living trust is to conduct a thorough inventory of all your assets. This includes everything you own, from real estate and bank accounts to personal property like vehicles, jewellery, and collectibles. A detailed inventory will help you understand the scope of your estate and ensure that all valuable items are accounted for.

Begin by listing all your real estate properties, including your primary residence, vacation homes, rental properties, and any other real estate holdings. Note the addresses, current market values, and any mortgages or liens attached to these properties. It's advisable to obtain professional appraisals to get accurate valuations, as real estate often constitutes a significant portion of an individual's assets.

Next, move on to your financial assets. This category includes checking and savings accounts, certificates of deposit (CDs), investment accounts, retirement accounts such as IRAs and 401(k)s, and any other financial instruments. For each account, record the account numbers, current balances, and the institutions where they are held. Keeping recent account statements handy will ensure that your information is up-to-date and accurate.

Personal property is another important category to consider. This includes valuable items such as cars, boats, art collections, antiques, and other collectibles. Document each item's description, estimated value, and any relevant identifying information, such as vehicle identification numbers (VINs) for cars or provenance details for art pieces. For high-value items, consider obtaining professional appraisals to ensure accurate valuations.

It's also essential to include intangible assets in your inventory. These might include patents, copyrights, trademarks, and business interests. If you own a business or have a stake in one, you need to document its value, your ownership percentage, and any relevant financial statements. Understanding the value of these intangible assets is crucial, as they can significantly impact the overall value of your estate.

Valuation of Assets

Once you have identified and listed all your assets, the next step is to determine their value. Accurate valuations are important for several reasons. They help in understanding the total worth of your estate, which is crucial for estate planning and tax purposes. They also provide a clear picture of what each beneficiary will receive, helping to avoid disputes and misunderstandings. For real estate, obtaining a professional appraisal is recommended. Appraisers use various methods to assess the value of a property, considering factors such as location, size, condition, and recent sales of similar properties in the area. An accurate appraisal ensures that the value of your real estate is correctly reflected in your trust. For financial accounts, use the most recent statements to get current balances. Investments can fluctuate in value, so it's important to regularly update these figures to reflect the latest market conditions. For retirement accounts, consider the potential tax implications of distributions, as these can affect the net value available to your beneficiaries. Valuing personal property can be more subjective, but professional appraisals can provide reliable estimates. For items such as jewellery, art, and collectibles, seek out experts in the respective fields. Their evaluations will be based on market trends, condition, rarity, and other relevant factors. For vehicles, you can use resources like the Kelley Blue Book to get an accurate estimate based on the make, model, year, and condition. Intangible assets, such as intellectual property and business interests, can be more complex to value. For intellectual property, consider potential future earnings from patents or trademarks. For business interests, a professional business valuation may be necessary. This process involves analysing financial statements, market conditions, and the overall health of the business to determine its worth.

Documentation and Record-Keeping

Maintaining thorough and accurate records of all your assets is essential for creating a reliable and effective living trust. Proper documentation not only ensures that all assets are correctly transferred into the trust but also provides a clear and organized record that can be easily referenced by your trustee and beneficiaries. Start by creating a comprehensive inventory document that lists all your assets, their values, and any relevant details. This document should be regularly updated to reflect any changes, such as the acquisition of new assets or changes in the value of existing ones. Keeping this document up to date is crucial, as it forms the backbone of your living trust. For real estate, keep copies of deeds, mortgage documents, and property tax assessments. These documents will be needed to transfer the property into the trust and to prove ownership and value. Ensure that all real estate transactions are properly recorded with the relevant authorities to avoid any legal complications. For financial accounts, maintain copies of recent statements, account agreements, and any other relevant documents. These will be necessary to change the ownership of the accounts to the trust. Regularly review your account statements to ensure that all information is accurate and up to date. Personal property should be documented with photographs, descriptions, and any relevant paperwork, such as purchase receipts or appraisals. For high-value items, keep appraisal reports and insurance documents handy. This documentation will be useful not only for transferring the items into the trust but also for insurance purposes. For intangible assets, gather any relevant documentation, such as intellectual property filings, business financial statements, and ownership agreements. These documents will help in accurately valuing and transferring these assets into the trust. Good record-keeping practices also involve keeping copies of your trust documents, including the trust deed, any amendments, and related correspondence. Store these documents in a safe place, such as a fireproof safe or a secure digital repository. Ensure that your trustee and key beneficiaries know where these documents are located and how to access them if necessary. By thoroughly assessing your assets, obtaining accurate valuations, and maintaining meticulous records, you lay a solid foundation for creating a living trust that effectively manages and protects your estate. This initial step is crucial, as it ensures that all your assets are accounted for and properly documented, paving the way for a smooth and efficient trust creation process

1.1 Assessing Your Assets

Assessing your assets is the cornerstone of creating an effective living trust. This process involves taking a thorough inventory of everything you own, determining the value of each asset, and ensuring proper documentation and record-keeping. By carefully evaluating your assets, you can make informed decisions about how to structure your living trust and distribute your estate according to your wishes.

Inventory of Personal and Real Property

The first step in assessing your assets is to compile a comprehensive list of everything you own. This includes both personal property and real property. Personal property encompasses movable items such as jewellery, vehicles, artwork, and collectibles, while real property refers to immovable assets like land and buildings.

Real Estate: List all real estate properties, including your primary residence, vacation homes, rental properties, and undeveloped land. Note the addresses, types of property, and current market values. Professional appraisals are advisable for accurate valuations.

Financial Assets: Include checking and savings accounts, certificates of deposit (CDs), stocks, bonds, mutual funds, retirement accounts (such as IRAs and 401(k)s), and any other investment accounts. Record account numbers, current balances, and financial institutions. Regularly update these balances to reflect recent market conditions.

Personal Property: Catalog valuable personal items, such as vehicles, jewellery, art collections, antiques, and collectibles. Provide descriptions, estimated values, and any identifying information like serial numbers for electronics or vehicle identification numbers (VINs) for cars. Professional appraisals for high-value items ensure accurate valuations.

Business Interests: Document details of any business ownership. Include the business name, ownership percentage, and relevant financial statements. Professional business valuations may be necessary for accurate assessments.

Intangible Assets: Include patents, copyrights, trademarks, and other intellectual property. Proper documentation and valuation of these assets are essential.

Valuation of Assets

Once you have a comprehensive inventory of your assets, the next step is to determine their value. Accurate valuations are essential for effective estate planning, as they help you understand the total worth of your estate and ensure fair distribution to your beneficiaries.

Real Estate Valuation: Obtain professional appraisals to determine the current market value of each property. Appraisers consider factors like location, size, condition, and recent sales of similar properties for accurate assessments.

Financial Asset Valuation: Use recent account statements to determine current balances. Regularly update these valuations to reflect market changes and ensure accurate estate planning.

Personal Property Valuation: Professional appraisals are recommended for valuable personal items. Appraisers consider factors like condition, rarity, and market demand for accurate valuations.

Business Valuation: Professional business valuations involve analysing financial statements, market conditions, and business health to determine value. This ensures fair distribution to beneficiaries.

Intangible Asset Valuation: Valuing intangible assets like intellectual property can be complex. Consider potential future earnings and consult with experts for accurate valuations.

Documentation and Record-Keeping

Maintaining thorough and accurate records of all your assets is crucial for creating a reliable and effective living trust. Proper documentation ensures that all assets are correctly transferred into the Trust and provides a clear and organized record for your trustee and beneficiaries.

Inventory Document: Create a comprehensive inventory document listing all your assets, values, and relevant details. Regularly update this document to reflect any changes. Keeping this document up to date is crucial for your living trust.

Real Estate Records: Keep copies of deeds, mortgage documents, and property tax assessments for all real estate properties. These documents are necessary for transferring the property into the trust and proving ownership and value. Ensure all transactions are recorded with relevant authorities.

Financial Account Statements: Maintain copies of recent statements, account agreements, and other relevant documents for financial accounts. These records are necessary for changing account ownership to the trust. Regularly review account statements for accuracy.

Personal Property Documentation: Document valuable personal items with photographs, descriptions, and relevant paperwork like purchase receipts or appraisals. Keep appraisal reports and insurance documents handy for high-value items.

Intangible Asset Documentation: Gather relevant documentation for intangible assets, like intellectual property filings, business financial statements, and ownership agreements. These documents help in accurately valuing and transferring assets into the trust.

Trust Documents: Keep copies of trust documents, including the trust deed, amendments, and related correspondence. Store these documents in a safe place, like a fireproof safe or secure digital repository. Ensure your trustee and key beneficiaries know where these documents are located and how to access them if necessary.

By thoroughly assessing your assets, obtaining accurate valuations, and maintaining meticulous records, you lay a solid foundation for creating a living trust that effectively manages and protects your estate. This initial step ensures all your assets are accounted for and properly documented, paving the way for a smooth and efficient trust creation process.

1.2 Choosing a Trustee: Criteria and Considerations

Selecting the right trustee is a critical decision when creating a living trust. The trustee's role involves managing the trust assets according to your wishes and ensuring the beneficiaries are taken care of. This section will guide you through the process of choosing a trustee, discussing the essential qualifications and characteristics to look for, the pros and cons of different types of trustees, and the importance of planning for successor trustees.

Qualifications and Characteristics of a Good Trustee

A trustee's responsibilities are complex and require various skills and qualities to manage the trust effectively. Here are some key qualifications and characteristics to consider:

Trustworthiness: The most crucial quality of a trustee is trustworthiness. This person will have control over your assets and be responsible for executing your wishes. Therefore, choose someone honest, reliable, and with a strong sense of integrity.

Financial Acumen: Managing a trust involves handling investments, paying bills, and making financial decisions. A trustee should have a good understanding of financial matters, including investment strategies, tax implications, and budgeting.

Attention to Detail: A trustee must be meticulous and organized, keeping accurate records of all transactions and decisions made on behalf of the trust. This attention to detail ensures the trust operates smoothly and beneficiaries receive what they are entitled to.

Impartiality: The trustee should act impartially, treating all beneficiaries fairly and without favouritism. This is particularly important in situations where the trustee is also a beneficiary or where there are potential conflicts of interest.

Communication Skills: Effective communication is essential for a trustee, who must regularly update beneficiaries, respond to their inquiries, and provide clear explanations of the trust's activities and decisions.

Availability: The trustee should have the time and willingness to dedicate to managing the trust. This responsibility can be time-consuming, so it's important that the trustee is both able and committed to fulfilling their duties.

Family Member vs. Professional Trustee

When choosing a trustee, you have the option of selecting a family member, a friend, or a professional trustee, such as a bank or a trust company. Each option has its advantages and disadvantages:

Family Member or Friend:

>   **Advantages:**

- Personal Knowledge: A family member or close friend may better understand your personal wishes and family dynamics.
- Cost: Typically, a family member or friend will not charge a fee for serving as trustee, which can save money.

Disadvantages:

Emotional Involvement: Managing a trust can be stressful, and a family member or friend may find it difficult to remain impartial, especially in the face of family conflicts.

Lack of Expertise: Unless they have a background in finance or law, a family member or friend may lack the necessary skills to manage the trust effectively.

Professional Trustee:

Advantages:

Expertise: Professional trustees, such as banks or trust companies, have experience and expertise in managing trusts, investments, and legal matters.

Impartiality: Professional trustees can act objectively and impartially, reducing the risk of family conflicts.

Continuity: Professional trustees can provide continuity and stability, as they are not affected by personal circumstances such as illness or death.

Disadvantages:

Cost: Professional trustees charge fees for their services, which can vary based on the complexity and size of the trust.

Personal Touch: Professional trustees may not have the same personal connection or understanding of your family's specific needs and dynamics.

Successor Trustees: Planning for Continuity

It is crucial to plan for continuity by naming one or more successor trustees in your trust document. A successor trustee will step in if the original trustee is unable or unwilling to serve. This ensures there is always someone in place to manage the trust and carry out your wishes.

Choosing Successor Trustees: When selecting successor trustees, consider individuals or institutions that possess the same qualities and qualifications as your primary trustee. It's a good idea to name multiple successor trustees in order of preference, providing a clear succession plan.

Documenting Succession Plans: Clearly document your succession plans in the trust agreement, specifying the circumstances under which a successor trustee should take over and the process for appointing them. This can help prevent confusion and disputes later on.

Communicating Your Plans: Ensure your primary trustee and all named successors are aware of their roles and responsibilities. Discuss your expectations and provide them with copies of the trust document. Open communication can help ensure a smooth transition if a successor trustee needs to step in.

Reviewing and Updating: Regularly review and update your choice of trustees and successor trustees as circumstances change. For example, if a named trustee is no longer available or suitable, update your trust document accordingly to reflect your current wishes.

By carefully choosing a trustee and planning for successor trustees, you can ensure that your living trust will be managed effectively and in accordance with your wishes. This thoughtful selection process helps safeguard your assets, provide for your beneficiaries, and maintain the integrity of your estate plan.

1.3 Drafting the Trust Document: A Step-by-Step Guide

Drafting the trust document is a crucial step in creating a living trust. This legal document outlines the terms and conditions of the trust, detailing how the trust should be managed and how the assets should be distributed to the beneficiaries. In this section, we will discuss the key clauses to include, how to customize the trust to fit your specific needs, and the legal considerations and language required to ensure the document is valid and effective.

Key Clauses to Include

When drafting your trust document, it is essential to include specific clauses that address the critical aspects of trust management and distribution. Here are some key clauses to consider:

Declaration of Trust: This clause establishes the trust and outlines the grantor's intent to create the trust. It should include the name of the trust, the date it is established, and the grantor's declaration that they are transferring assets into the trust.

Identification of Parties: Clearly identify the grantor, trustee, and beneficiaries in the trust document. This section should include the full names and addresses of all parties involved.

Powers and Duties of the Trustee: Define the powers and responsibilities of the trustee. This clause should detail the trustee's authority to manage, invest, and distribute the trust assets, as well as any limitations on their powers.

Distribution of Assets: Specify how the trust assets should be distributed to the beneficiaries. This clause should include the conditions and timing of distributions, such as age-specific distributions for minor beneficiaries or specific events that trigger distributions.

Incapacity Provisions: Include provisions for managing the trust in the event the grantor becomes incapacitated. This clause should outline the process for determining incapacity and the procedures for the successor trustee to take over management of the trust.

Amendment and Revocation: Describe the procedures for amending or revoking the trust. This clause should specify under what conditions the grantor can make changes to the trust and how those changes should be documented.

Successor Trustee: Identify the successor trustees who will take over if the primary trustee is unable or unwilling to serve. This clause should also detail the process for appointing successor trustees.

Spendthrift Provision: Protect the trust assets from creditors of the beneficiaries by including a spendthrift provision. This clause prevents beneficiaries from transferring or pledging their interest in the trust assets to creditors.

No-Contest Clause: To minimize the risk of disputes among beneficiaries, consider including a no-contest clause. This provision can disinherit any beneficiary who challenges the validity of the trust.

Customizing the Trust to Fit Your Needs

Every individual's situation is unique, and your trust document should reflect your specific needs and wishes. Customizing the trust allows you to include specific instructions for the management and distribution of your assets, provisions for special needs beneficiaries, and other personalized elements.

Specific Bequests: If you want to leave specific items or amounts of money to beneficiaries, include these specific bequests in the trust document. Clearly describe the items or amounts and identify the beneficiaries who will receive them.

Special Needs Trust: If you have a beneficiary with special needs, consider creating a special needs trust within your living trust. This provision ensures that the beneficiary receives the necessary support without jeopardizing their eligibility for government benefits.

Charitable Contributions: If you wish to leave a portion of your estate to charity, include provisions for charitable contributions in the trust document. Specify the charities you want to support and the amounts or percentages of your estate they should receive.

Pet Trust: If you have pets, you may want to include a pet trust provision to ensure they are cared for after your death. This clause should specify who will take care of your pets and how funds should be allocated for their care.

Legal Considerations and Language

Using clear and precise legal language in your trust document is essential to avoid ambiguities and potential disputes. Here are some legal considerations to keep in mind:

State Laws: Trust laws vary by state, so it is important to ensure that your trust document complies with the laws of your state. Consulting with an estate planning attorney who is familiar with your state's laws can help ensure that your trust is valid and enforceable.

Witnesses and Notarization: Depending on your state's requirements, your trust document may need to be witnessed and notarized. This adds an extra layer of validity and helps prevent challenges to the trust's authenticity.

Clear Definitions: Use clear and unambiguous language to define key terms and provisions in the trust document. This helps ensure that the trustee and beneficiaries understand your intentions and can follow your instructions accurately.

Legal Counsel: While it is possible to create a trust document using online templates, consulting with an experienced estate planning attorney is highly recommended. An attorney can provide personalized advice, ensure that your trust meets all legal requirements, and help you avoid common pitfalls.

By including these key clauses, customizing the trust to fit your needs, and ensuring the document meets legal standards, you can create a comprehensive and effective trust document. This document will serve as the foundation for managing and distributing your assets according to your wishes, providing peace of mind for you and your beneficiaries.

Chapter 2: Necessary Documentation

Creating a living trust involves more than just drafting the trust document. To ensure your trust is legally valid and effective, you need to gather and prepare several essential pieces of documentation. This chapter will guide you through the necessary documentation required to establish, fund, and maintain your living trust. By carefully preparing these documents, you can avoid common pitfalls and ensure that your trust operates smoothly.

Trust Deed

The trust deed, also known as the trust agreement, is the foundational document of your living trust. It outlines the terms and conditions under which the trust operates, including the roles and responsibilities of the grantor, trustee, and beneficiaries. Key elements of the trust deed include:

Declaration of Trust: This section establishes the trust and includes the grantor's intent to create the trust. It should specify the name of the trust, the date it is established, and a statement that the grantor is transferring assets into the trust.

Identification of Parties: Clearly identify the grantor, trustee, and beneficiaries. This section should include their full names and addresses. It is essential to be precise to avoid any confusion or disputes later.

Trustee's Powers and Duties: Detail the powers and responsibilities of the trustee. This includes the authority to manage, invest, and distribute the trust assets. Specify any limitations on the trustee's powers to ensure they act within the scope of their authority.

Distribution Provisions: Specify how the trust assets will be distributed to the beneficiaries. This section should include conditions and timing of distributions, such as age-specific distributions for minors or specific events that trigger distributions.

Incapacity Provisions: Outline procedures for managing the trust if the grantor becomes incapacitated. This section should define how incapacity is determined and the process for the successor trustee to take over management of the trust.

Amendment and Revocation: Describe the procedures for amending or revoking the trust. Specify under what conditions the grantor can make changes and how those changes should be documented.

Successor Trustee Provisions: Identify successor trustees who will take over if the original trustee cannot serve. Detail the process for appointing successor trustees to ensure a smooth transition.

Spendthrift Clause: Include a spendthrift clause to protect the trust assets from creditors of the beneficiaries. This clause prevents beneficiaries from pledging or transferring their interest in the trust to creditors.

No-Contest Clause: To minimize disputes, consider a no-contest clause. This provision can disinherit any beneficiary who challenges the validity of the trust.

Declaration of Trust

The declaration of trust is a formal statement expressing the grantor's intent to create the trust and transfer assets into it. It is a critical part of establishing the trust's legal validity. This document should include:

Grantor's Intent: Clearly state the grantor's intent to create a trust and transfer assets into it. This declaration should be unequivocal to prevent any challenges to the trust's validity.

Asset Transfer: List the assets being transferred into the trust. This section should be comprehensive, covering all real estate, financial accounts, personal property, and other assets included in the trust.

Witnesses and Notarization: Depending on your state's requirements, the declaration of trust may need to be witnessed and notarized. This adds an extra layer of legal validity and helps prevent challenges to the document's authenticity.

Funding the Trust

Funding the trust involves transferring ownership of your assets into the trust. This step is crucial to ensure that the trust operates effectively, and the assets are managed according to the terms of the trust. Here are the primary steps and documentation required:

Real Estate: To transfer real estate into the trust, you need to execute a new deed transferring ownership from yourself to the trust. This deed must be recorded with the local county recorder's office. Ensure that the deed is properly drafted and meets all legal requirements to avoid any issues with property transfer.

Financial Accounts: Change the title of your financial accounts, such as checking and savings accounts, investment accounts, and retirement accounts, to reflect the trust as the new owner. This typically involves completing forms provided by the financial institutions holding the accounts. Keep copies of all completed forms and account statements showing the change of ownership.

Personal Property: For valuable personal items, create an assignment of ownership document transferring the items to the trust. This document should be detailed and include descriptions, serial numbers, and appraised values. Keep copies of any relevant purchase receipts, appraisals, and insurance documents.

Business Interests: If you own a business or have a stake in one, you may need to amend the ownership documents to reflect the trust as the new owner. This could involve updating the business's operating agreement or issuing new stock certificates. Consult with a legal professional to ensure the transfer complies with all applicable laws and regulations.

Intellectual Property: Transfer ownership of patents, trademarks, copyrights, and other intellectual property into the trust. This may involve filing new ownership documents with the appropriate government agencies. Ensure that all filings are accurate and complete to avoid any issues with intellectual property rights.

Maintaining the Trust

Once your trust is established and funded, it is essential to maintain it properly to ensure its ongoing effectiveness. This involves regular reviews and updates, as well as diligent record-keeping.

Regular Reviews: Periodically review your trust to ensure it continues to meet your needs and reflects your current wishes. Life events such as marriage, divorce, the birth of a child, or significant changes in your financial situation may necessitate updates to the trust.

Updating the Trust: Make any necessary amendments to the trust document to reflect changes in your circumstances or wishes. Ensure that all amendments are documented properly and, if required, witnessed and notarized.

Record-Keeping: Maintain thorough and accurate records of all transactions and changes related to the trust. This includes keeping copies of the trust deed, amendments, asset transfer documents, account statements, and any correspondence related to the trust. Organized record-keeping helps ensure the trust operates smoothly and provides a clear record for the trustee and beneficiaries.

Communication with Trustee and Beneficiaries: Keep the trustee and beneficiaries informed about the trust's status and any significant changes.

Clear communication helps prevent misunderstandings and ensures that everyone involved understands their roles and responsibilities.

By carefully preparing and maintaining the necessary documentation for your living trust, you can ensure that your estate is managed and distributed according to your wishes. Proper documentation provides legal validity to the trust, helps prevent disputes, and ensures a smooth and efficient administration of the trust assets.

2.1 Trust Deed: Key Elements

The trust deed, also known as the trust agreement, is the cornerstone document of your living trust. It establishes the trust, outlines the terms under which it operates, and details the roles and responsibilities of all parties involved. Crafting a thorough and precise trust deed is essential to ensure that your trust functions as intended and meets all legal requirements.

Purpose and Structure of the Trust Deed

The trust deed serves as the legal framework for your living trust. It should be comprehensive and clearly written to avoid any ambiguities or misunderstandings. The structure of the trust deed typically includes the following sections:

Title and Declaration of Trust: This section formally establishes the trust, including the name of the trust and the date of its creation. It should clearly state the grantor's intention to create the trust and transfer assets into it.

Identification of Parties: This section identifies the key parties involved in the trust, including the grantor (the person creating the trust), the trustee (the person or entity managing the trust), and the beneficiaries (the individuals or organizations benefiting from the trust). Full names and addresses should be included to ensure clear identification.

Trustee's Powers and Duties: Detail the powers granted to the trustee to manage the trust assets. This section should include specific responsibilities, such as investing assets, making distributions to beneficiaries, and handling administrative tasks. It should also outline any limitations on the trustee's authority to ensure they act within the scope of their role.

Distribution Provisions: Specify how and when the trust assets will be distributed to the beneficiaries. This section should include any conditions or milestones that must be met before distributions are made, such as the beneficiary reaching a certain age or achieving a particular goal.

Incapacity Provisions: Include provisions for managing the trust in the event the grantor becomes incapacitated. This section should outline how incapacity is determined and the process for the successor trustee to take over management of the trust.

Amendment and Revocation: Describe the procedures for amending or revoking the trust. This section should specify under what conditions the grantor can make changes to the trust and how those changes should be documented.

Successor Trustee Provisions: Identify the successor trustees who will take over if the original trustee is unable or unwilling to serve. This section should also detail the process for appointing successor trustees to ensure a smooth transition.

Spendthrift Clause: Include a spendthrift clause to protect the trust assets from creditors of the beneficiaries. This clause prevents beneficiaries from pledging or transferring their interest in the trust to creditors, ensuring the assets remain within the trust for their intended purpose.

No-Contest Clause: To minimize disputes among beneficiaries, consider including a no-contest clause. This provision can disinherit any beneficiary who challenges the validity of the trust, discouraging legal battles and promoting harmony among beneficiaries.

Essential Provisions and Clauses

In addition to the standard sections, your trust deed should include several essential provisions and clauses to address specific circumstances and provide clarity on key issues:

Tax Provisions: Address the tax implications of the trust, including any strategies to minimize estate and income taxes. This section should outline the responsibilities of the trustee in managing tax matters and ensuring compliance with applicable tax laws.

Administrative Provisions: Include provisions for the ongoing administration of the trust, such as the frequency of trustee reports to beneficiaries, the process for handling expenses and fees, and the procedures for record-keeping and documentation.

Guardianship Provisions: If the trust includes provisions for minor beneficiaries, include guardianship provisions to designate who will manage the assets on behalf of the minors until they reach adulthood. This ensures that the minors' interests are protected and managed responsibly.

Charitable Provisions: If the trust includes charitable contributions, specify the charities or causes you wish to support and the amounts or percentages of your estate they should receive. This section should also address any conditions or restrictions on the use of the funds.

Environmental and Ethical Considerations: Include any specific instructions or preferences regarding the management of trust assets in line with your environmental or ethical values. For example, you might specify that investments should be made in socially responsible funds or that certain types of investments should be avoided.

Common Mistakes to Avoid

Drafting a trust deed requires careful attention to detail to avoid common mistakes that can undermine the effectiveness of your trust. Here are some pitfalls to watch out for:

Vague Language: Ambiguities in the trust deed can lead to misunderstandings and disputes. Use clear, precise language and define key terms to ensure that your intentions are clearly understood.

Lack of Specificity: Be specific about the roles and responsibilities of the trustee and the conditions for distributions to beneficiaries. General or vague instructions can create confusion and make it difficult for the trustee to administer the trust effectively.

Ignoring State Laws: Trust laws vary by state, so it is crucial to ensure that your trust deed complies with the laws of your state. Consulting with an estate planning attorney familiar with your state's laws can help ensure that your trust is legally valid and enforceable.

Inadequate Successor Planning: Failing to name successor trustees or provide clear instructions for their appointment can lead to complications if the original trustee is unable to serve. Ensure that your trust deed includes a detailed plan for successor trustees to avoid disruptions in trust management

Overlooking Tax Implications: Neglecting to address the tax implications of the trust can result in unnecessary tax burdens for the trust and beneficiaries. Include provisions for tax planning and compliance to minimize tax liabilities.

By including these key elements, provisions, and clauses in your trust deed, you can create a comprehensive and effective document that ensures your living trust operates smoothly and according to your wishes. Properly drafting the trust deed is essential to protect your assets, provide for your beneficiaries, and maintain the integrity of your estate plan.

2.2 Declaration of Trust: Importance and Contents

The declaration of trust is a critical document in the creation of your living trust. It serves as a formal statement that articulates your intent to establish the trust and transfer assets into it. This document not only provides legal validation of your trust but also ensures clarity and precision in the administration and distribution of your estate. Crafting a well-defined declaration of trust helps prevent future disputes and guarantees that your wishes are honoured.

Importance of the Declaration of Trust

The declaration of trust plays several pivotal roles in the establishment and operation of your living trust:

Legal Validation: A clearly articulated declaration of trust serves as legal evidence of your intent to create the trust and transfer your assets into it. This helps in establishing the trust's authenticity and enforceability, protecting it from potential challenges.

Clarity of Intent: The declaration explicitly states your goals and wishes regarding the management and distribution of your assets. This clarity is crucial for guiding the trustee and preventing misunderstandings or disputes among beneficiaries.

Documentation of Assets: Including a detailed list of the assets being transferred into the trust ensures that all property is accounted for and properly managed. This documentation is vital for effective trust administration and asset protection.

27

Contents of the Declaration of Trust

A comprehensive declaration of trust should contain several key elements to ensure its effectiveness and legal standing:

Grantor's Intent: Begin with a clear statement of your intention to create a living trust and transfer assets into it. This declaration should leave no room for ambiguity. For example: "I, [Your Full Name], hereby declare that I am creating a living trust named [Trust's Name], dated [Date], and transferring the assets listed below into this trust."

Name of the Trust: Specify the official name of the trust. This name will be used in all related legal and financial documents. Including the date of the trust's creation in the name can add clarity, such as "The [Your Last Name] Family Trust dated [Date]."

Identification of Parties: Clearly identify all parties involved in the trust. This includes the grantor (yourself), the trustee, any successor trustees, and the beneficiaries. Use full names and addresses to ensure precise identification and avoid future disputes.

Asset Transfer: Provide a detailed list of the assets being transferred into the trust. This should cover all types of assets, such as real estate, financial accounts, personal property, business interests, and intellectual property. For each asset, include specific details like addresses for real estate, account numbers for financial assets, and descriptions for personal property.

Trustee's Powers and Duties: Outline the powers and responsibilities of the trustee in managing the trust assets. This section should specify the trustee's authority to invest assets, make distributions, and handle administrative tasks, as well as any limitations on their powers.

Distribution Provisions: Detail how the trust assets will be distributed to the beneficiaries. This section should include any conditions or milestones that must be met before distributions are made, such as age-specific distributions for minors or specific events that trigger distributions.

Incapacity Provisions: Include provisions for managing the trust in the event of your incapacity. Outline how incapacity is determined and the process for the successor trustee to assume management of the trust. These provisions ensure continuous and proper management of your assets.

Amendment and Revocation: Describe the procedures for amending or revoking the trust. Specify the conditions under which you can make changes to the trust and the process for documenting these changes. This section provides flexibility to adapt the trust as circumstances change.

Witnesses and Notarization: Depending on your state's requirements, the declaration of trust may need to be witnessed and notarized. Having witnesses and a notary signature adds an extra layer of legal validation and helps prevent challenges to the document's authenticity.

Sample Declaration of Trust

Here is a sample template to illustrate the structure and content of a declaration of trust:

Declaration of Trust

I, *[Your Full Name]*, residing at *[Your Address],* hereby declare this living trust, named *[Trust's Name],* dated [*Date*].

I appoint myself as the initial trustee of this trust. If I am unable or unwilling to serve, I appoint [Successor Trustee's Full Name] as my successor trustee.

I transfer the following assets into this trust:

Real Estate: *[Property Address, Legal Description]*

Financial Accounts: *[Bank Name, Account Number, Current Balance]*

Personal Property: *[Description, Estimated Value]*

Business Interests: *[Business Name, Ownership Percentage]*

Intellectual Property: *[Description, Registration Number]*

The trustee shall have the powers to manage, invest, and distribute the trust assets according to the terms outlined in this document. Distributions to beneficiaries shall be made as follows:

[Beneficiary's Full Name], [Relationship], shall receive [Percentage or Specific Amount], upon reaching [Age or Condition].

In the event of my incapacity, as determined by [Method of Determination], the successor trustee shall take over management of the trust.

This trust may be amended or revoked by me at any time, provided such amendments or revocations are documented in writing and signed by me.

This declaration is made on [*Date*] in the presence of the undersigned witnesses and notarized by *[Notary's Name]*.

[Your Signature]

[Witness Signature 1]

[Witness Signature 2]

[Notary Signature and Seal]

By including these essential elements and clearly outlining your intentions, you can create a comprehensive and effective declaration of trust. This document serves as the foundation for your living trust, ensuring that your assets are managed and distributed according to your wishes.

2.3 Designation of Beneficiaries: Criteria for Selection

Designating beneficiaries is one of the most critical aspects of creating a living trust. This process involves carefully selecting the individuals or organizations who will benefit from your trust and outlining the terms and conditions of their inheritance. Clear, thoughtful designations help ensure your assets are distributed according to your wishes and minimize the potential for disputes among beneficiaries. This section will guide you through identifying primary and contingent beneficiaries, considerations for minors and special needs beneficiaries, and the importance of updating beneficiary designations over time.

Identifying Primary and Contingent Beneficiaries

When designating beneficiaries, it's important to distinguish between primary and contingent beneficiaries. Primary beneficiaries are the main recipients of the trust assets, while contingent beneficiaries receive assets only if the primary beneficiaries are unable or unwilling to do so.

Primary Beneficiaries: These individuals or organizations are your first choice for receiving the trust assets. Clearly identify each primary beneficiary by their full name and, if applicable, their relationship to you. Specify the portion of the trust they are entitled to receive, which can be expressed as a percentage or a specific amount.

Contingent Beneficiaries: These beneficiaries' step in if a primary beneficiary predeceases you, declines the inheritance, or is otherwise unable to receive the assets. Like primary beneficiaries, contingent beneficiaries should be clearly identified with their full names and the conditions under which they will inherit. This ensures that there is a backup plan in place, providing security and clarity for the distribution of your estate.

Considerations for Minors and Special Needs Beneficiaries

Special considerations are necessary when naming minors or individuals with special needs as beneficiaries. These beneficiaries may require additional provisions to ensure their inheritance is managed appropriately and does not negatively impact their eligibility for government benefits.

Minors: Minors cannot legally manage significant financial assets. Therefore, it's essential to include provisions that designate a guardian or trustee to manage the inheritance on their behalf until they reach the age of majority. Consider setting up a trust within your living trust specifically for minor beneficiaries. This sub-trust can outline the terms of how and when the funds should be used, such as for education, healthcare, and general living expenses, and when the beneficiary will gain full control of the assets.

Special Needs Beneficiaries: Individuals with special needs may be eligible for government benefits that are means-tested. Receiving a large inheritance outright could jeopardize their eligibility for these benefits. To prevent this, consider setting up a special needs trust within your living trust. This type of trust allows the beneficiary to receive the benefits of the trust without directly owning the assets, thereby preserving their eligibility for government assistance. The special needs trust should be carefully drafted to comply with federal and state laws, ensuring that it effectively meets the beneficiary's needs without adverse consequences.

Updating Beneficiaries Over Time

Life circumstances change, and it is crucial to review and update your beneficiary designations periodically. Failing to update your beneficiaries can lead to unintended consequences, such as assets being distributed to individuals you no longer wish to benefit or to an outdated address.

Regular Reviews: Make it a habit to review your beneficiary designations at least annually or after major life events. Events such as marriage, divorce, the birth of a child, or the death of a named beneficiary should prompt an immediate review and update of your trust documents. Regular reviews help ensure that your trust remains aligned with your current wishes and family dynamics.

Clear Documentation: Whenever you make changes to your beneficiary designations, document these changes clearly and thoroughly. Amend the trust document to reflect the new designations and ensure that the changes are properly witnessed and notarized if required by state law. This prevents confusion and potential disputes among beneficiaries.

Communication with Beneficiaries: While it's not always necessary to inform beneficiaries of their status, clear communication can help manage expectations and reduce the potential for disputes. If appropriate, discuss your intentions with your beneficiaries so they understand your wishes and the reasons behind your decisions. This transparency can foster better relationships and reduce the likelihood of conflicts after your passing.

Coordination with Other Estate Planning Documents: Ensure that the beneficiary designations in your living trust are consistent with other estate planning documents, such as your will, life insurance policies, and retirement accounts. Inconsistent designations can lead to confusion and legal challenges, potentially delaying the distribution of your assets. A comprehensive review of all your estate planning documents can help ensure consistency and avoid conflicts.

By carefully selecting and regularly updating your beneficiaries, you can ensure that your living trust accurately reflects your wishes and provides for your loved ones in the manner you intend. Clear designations and thoughtful planning help to prevent disputes, protect vulnerable beneficiaries, and ensure that your estate is managed and distributed according to your wishes.

Chapter 3: Funding the Trust

Creating a living trust is a significant step in estate planning, but its effectiveness depends on properly funding it. Funding the trust involves transferring ownership of your assets into the trust, ensuring that they are managed and distributed according to your wishes. This chapter will guide you through the process of funding your trust, covering the transfer of real estate, financial accounts, personal property, business interests, and intellectual property. Properly funding your trust is essential to protect your assets and ensure they are managed according to the terms of the trust.

Transferring Real Estate

Real estate often represents a significant portion of an individual's assets and requires careful handling when transferring ownership to a trust. The process involves preparing a new deed that transfers the property's title from your name to the trust's name. Here's how to do it:

Prepare the Deed: A new deed must be drafted to transfer the property title to the trust. This deed can be a warranty deed, quitclaim deed, or grant deed, depending on your state's requirements and the type of property transfer. The deed should include the legal description of the property, the grantor's name (your name), and the grantee's name (the name of your trust).

Sign and Notarize the Deed: The deed must be signed by you (the grantor) and notarized to be legally binding. Notarization provides an additional layer of authentication and prevents disputes about the validity of the document.

Record the Deed: The notarized deed should be recorded with the county recorder's office in the jurisdiction where the property is located. Recording the deed makes the transfer a matter of public record, which is necessary to establish the trust's ownership of the property. Pay any required recording fees and ensure that the county records are updated to reflect the new ownership.

Update Insurance Policies: Once the property is transferred to the trust, update any related insurance policies to reflect the new ownership. This includes homeowners' insurance and title insurance. Ensuring that the trust is listed as the insured party helps protect the property and the trust's interests.

Transferring Financial Accounts

Financial accounts, such as bank accounts, investment accounts, and retirement accounts, also need to be transferred into the trust. The process varies depending on the type of account and the financial institution, but generally involves the following steps:

Contact Financial Institutions: Reach out to the banks, brokerage firms, and other financial institutions where you hold accounts. Inform them of your intention to transfer ownership to your living trust and request the necessary forms to complete the transfer.

Complete Transfer Forms: Fill out the forms provided by the financial institutions. These forms typically require information about the trust, including the trust's name, date of creation, and the trustee's name. Some institutions may require a copy of the trust agreement or a certification of trust.

Change Account Titles: Update the account titles to reflect the trust's ownership. For example, a bank account in your name would be retitled to "[Your Name], Trustee of [Your Trust's Name], dated [Trust's Date]". Ensure that all accounts are correctly retitled to avoid confusion and ensure that the trust owns the assets.

Update Beneficiary Designations: For retirement accounts and other accounts with beneficiary designations, ensure that the designations align with your overall estate plan. You may need to update the beneficiary to the trust or confirm that the designations reflect your current wishes.

Transferring Personal Property

Personal property, including valuable items such as vehicles, jewellery, artwork, and collectibles, should also be transferred into the trust. This process generally involves creating a written assignment of ownership and maintaining accurate records:

Create an Assignment of Ownership: Draft a document that assigns ownership of your personal property to the trust. This assignment should list each item being transferred, providing detailed descriptions and any relevant identifying information (e.g., serial numbers or VINs for vehicles). Include the date of the transfer and your signature as the grantor.

Update Titles and Registrations: For items that have titles or registrations, such as vehicles and boats, update the titles to reflect the trust's ownership. Contact the appropriate government agencies to complete the necessary paperwork and pay any associated fees.

Maintain Records: Keep copies of the assignment of ownership, updated titles, and any related documentation. This helps ensure that there is a clear record of the trust's ownership of your personal property, which is important for both legal and practical purposes.

Transferring Business Interests

If you own a business or have a stake in one, transferring your business interests into the trust is essential to ensure continuity and proper management:

Review Ownership Agreements: Examine the business's ownership agreements, such as partnership agreements, operating agreements, or shareholder agreements. These documents may have specific provisions regarding the transfer of ownership interests, including any restrictions or required approvals.

Prepare Transfer Documents: Draft the necessary documents to transfer your business interests to the trust. This may include updating the operating agreement, issuing new stock certificates, or amending partnership agreements. Consult with a legal professional to ensure compliance with all applicable laws and the business's governing documents.

Notify Business Partners: Inform your business partners of the transfer and provide them with copies of the updated ownership documents. Clear communication helps prevent misunderstandings and ensures that everyone is aware of the new ownership structure.

Record the Transfer: Ensure that the transfer is properly recorded in the business's records. Update the company's books, stock ledger, or partnership records to reflect the trust's ownership of your business interests.

Transferring Intellectual Property

Intellectual property, such as patents, trademarks, copyrights, and other proprietary rights, should also be transferred to the trust to ensure proper management and protection:

Identify Intellectual Property: Make a comprehensive list of all intellectual property you own, including detailed descriptions and any relevant registration numbers or documentation.

Prepare Transfer Documents: Draft the necessary documents to assign ownership of your intellectual property to the trust. This may include assignment agreements, transfer deeds, or other legal instruments required to effectuate the transfer.

File with Relevant Authorities: For registered intellectual property, such as patents and trademarks, file the assignment documents with the appropriate government agencies. This ensures that the trust is recognized as the new owner and maintains the legal protections associated with the intellectual property.

Maintain Records: Keep copies of all assignment documents, filings, and related correspondence. Proper record-keeping helps protect your intellectual property rights and ensures that the trust can manage these assets effectively.

Properly funding your trust is a critical step in ensuring that your estate plan is effective and that your assets are managed and distributed according to your wishes. By carefully transferring ownership of your real estate, financial accounts, personal property, business interests, and intellectual property into the trust, you can protect your assets and provide clear guidance for your trustee and beneficiaries.

3.1 Transferring Assets into the Trust

Funding your living trust is an essential step in ensuring its effectiveness. Without proper funding, the trust cannot operate as intended, and your assets may not be managed or distributed according to your wishes. This section will guide you through the detailed process of transferring different types of assets into your living trust, ensuring a comprehensive and legally sound approach.

Transferring Real Estate

Real estate often represents a significant portion of an individual's assets and requires careful handling when transferring ownership to a trust. The process involves preparing and recording a new deed that transfers the property's title from your name to the trust's name.

Prepare the Deed: A new deed must be drafted to transfer the property title to the trust. This deed can be a warranty deed, quitclaim deed, or grant deed, depending on your state's requirements and the type of property transfer. The deed should include the legal description of the property, the grantor's name (your name), and the grantee's name (the name of your trust).

Sign and Notarize the Deed: The deed must be signed by you (the grantor) and notarized to be legally binding. Notarization provides an additional layer of authentication and prevents disputes about the validity of the document.

Record the Deed: The notarized deed should be recorded with the county recorder's office in the jurisdiction where the property is located. Recording the deed makes the transfer a matter of public record, which is necessary to establish the trust's ownership of the property. Pay any required recording fees and ensure that the county records are updated to reflect the new ownership.

Update Insurance Policies: Once the property is transferred to the trust, update any related insurance policies to reflect the new ownership. This includes homeowners' insurance and title insurance. Ensuring that the trust is listed as the insured party helps protect the property and the trust's interests.

Transferring Financial Accounts

Financial accounts, such as bank accounts, investment accounts, and retirement accounts, also need to be transferred into the trust. The process varies depending on the type of account and the financial institution, but generally involves the following steps:

Contact Financial Institutions: Reach out to the banks, brokerage firms, and other financial institutions where you hold accounts. Inform them of your intention to transfer ownership to your living trust and request the necessary forms to complete the transfer.

Complete Transfer Forms: Fill out the forms provided by the financial institutions. These forms typically require information about the trust, including the trust's name, date of creation, and the trustee's name. Some institutions may require a copy of the trust agreement or a certification of trust.

Change Account Titles: Update the account titles to reflect the trust's ownership. For example, a bank account in your name would be retitled to "[Your Name], Trustee of [Your Trust's Name], dated [Trust's Date]". Ensure that all accounts are correctly retitled to avoid confusion and ensure that the trust owns the assets.

Update Beneficiary Designations: For retirement accounts and other accounts with beneficiary designations, ensure that the designations align with your overall estate plan. You may need to update the beneficiary to the trust or confirm that the designations reflect your current wishes.

Transferring Personal Property

Personal property, including valuable items such as vehicles, jewellery, artwork, and collectibles, should also be transferred into the trust. This process generally involves creating a written assignment of ownership and maintaining accurate records:

Create an Assignment of Ownership: Draft a document that assigns ownership of your personal property to the trust. This assignment should list each item being transferred, providing detailed descriptions and any relevant identifying information (e.g., serial numbers or VINs for vehicles). Include the date of the transfer and your signature as the grantor.

Update Titles and Registrations: For items that have titles or registrations, such as vehicles and boats, update the titles to reflect the trust's ownership. Contact the appropriate government agencies to complete the necessary paperwork and pay any associated fees.

Maintain Records: Keep copies of the assignment of ownership, updated titles, and any related documentation. This helps ensure that there is a clear record of the trust's ownership of your personal property, which is important for both legal and practical purposes.

Transferring Business Interests

If you own a business or have a stake in one, transferring your business interests into the trust is essential to ensure continuity and proper management:

Review Ownership Agreements: Examine the business's ownership agreements, such as partnership agreements, operating agreements, or shareholder agreements. These documents may have specific provisions regarding the transfer of ownership interests, including any restrictions or required approvals.

Prepare Transfer Documents: Draft the necessary documents to transfer your business interests to the trust. This may include updating the operating agreement, issuing new stock certificates, or amending partnership agreements. Consult with a legal professional to ensure compliance with all applicable laws and the business's governing documents.

Notify Business Partners: Inform your business partners of the transfer and provide them with copies of the updated ownership documents. Clear communication helps prevent misunderstandings and ensures that everyone is aware of the new ownership structure.

Record the Transfer: Ensure that the transfer is properly recorded in the business's records. Update the company's books, stock ledger, or partnership records to reflect the trust's ownership of your business interests.

Transferring Intellectual Property

Intellectual property, such as patents, trademarks, copyrights, and other proprietary rights, should also be transferred to the trust to ensure proper management and protection:

Identify Intellectual Property: Make a comprehensive list of all intellectual property you own, including detailed descriptions and any relevant registration numbers or documentation.

Prepare Transfer Documents: Draft the necessary documents to assign ownership of your intellectual property to the trust. This may include assignment agreements, transfer deeds, or other legal instruments required to effectuate the transfer.

File with Relevant Authorities: For registered intellectual property, such as patents and trademarks, file the assignment documents with the appropriate government agencies. This ensures that the trust is recognized as the new owner and maintains the legal protections associated with the intellectual property.

Maintain Records: Keep copies of all assignment documents, filings, and related correspondence. Proper record-keeping helps protect your intellectual property rights and ensures that the trust can manage these assets effectively.

Ensuring Comprehensive Funding

For a living trust to function as intended, it must be fully funded. This means that all significant assets should be transferred into the trust. The process of funding the trust requires attention to detail and careful planning to avoid overlooking any assets. Regular reviews of your trust's funding status can help ensure that it remains comprehensive and up to date.

Conduct a Final Review: After transferring your assets, conduct a final review to ensure that all intended assets have been successfully transferred to the trust. This review should include verifying that all deeds, titles, account changes, and assignment documents are properly executed and recorded.

Periodic Updates: Regularly update the trust to reflect any new assets acquired or changes in your financial situation. This includes adding new properties, accounts, or valuable personal items to the trust. Keeping your trust current ensures that it continues to meet your estate planning goals.

Consult with Professionals: Work with estate planning professionals, such as attorneys and financial advisors, to ensure that all transfers are correctly executed and that the trust remains compliant with state laws and regulations. Professional guidance can help you navigate complex asset transfers and address any legal or tax implications.

By thoroughly transferring your assets into your living trust, you can ensure that your estate plan is effective and that your assets are managed and distributed according to your wishes. Properly funding the trust protects your assets, provides clear guidance for your trustee, and helps achieve your estate planning objectives.

3.2 Required Legal Documentation

Funding your trust involves more than just transferring assets; it requires meticulous attention to legal documentation to ensure that all transfers are legally valid and enforceable. Proper documentation protects your trust from legal challenges and ensures that your assets are correctly managed and distributed according to your wishes.

Transfer Forms and Procedures

Different types of assets require different forms and procedures for transfer. Here's a breakdown of the most common asset types and the required documentation:

Real Estate: To transfer real estate into the trust, you need to execute a new deed, such as a warranty deed, quitclaim deed, or grant deed. This deed must be properly drafted to include:

The legal description of the property.

The name of the grantor (your name).

The name of the grantee (the trust's name).

Signatures of the grantor and a notary public.

Once the deed is executed, it must be recorded with the county recorder's office in the jurisdiction where the property is located. Recording the deed ensures that the transfer is legally recognized and provides public notice of the change in ownership.

Financial Accounts: Transferring financial accounts to the trust typically involves completing forms provided by the financial institution. These forms will request:

The trust's name and date of creation.

The trustee's name and contact information.

A certification of trust or a copy of the trust agreement.

Once the forms are completed, the financial institution will update the account titles to reflect the trust's ownership. Keep copies of all submitted forms and updated account statements for your records.

Personal Property: For personal property, such as vehicles, jewellery, and artwork, a written assignment of ownership is usually required. This assignment should:

List each item being transferred with detailed descriptions.

Include relevant identifying information (e.g., serial numbers, VINs).

Be signed and dated by the grantor.

For vehicles and boats, update the titles through the appropriate government agency, such as the Department of Motor Vehicles (DMV). Ensure that the new titles reflect the trust's ownership.

Business Interests: Transferring business interests may involve updating the business's operating agreements, issuing new stock certificates, or amending partnership agreements. Required documentation may include:

An assignment of ownership interest to the trust.

Updated ownership records in the company's books.

Notification to business partners and relevant stakeholders.

Intellectual Property: To transfer intellectual property, such as patents and trademarks, you will need to prepare assignment agreements. These agreements should be filed with the relevant government agencies, ensuring that the trust is recognized as the new owner. Maintain copies of all assignment agreements and filings.

Notarization and Recordation

Notarization and recordation add layers of legal validity to your asset transfers, ensuring that they are recognized and enforceable. Here's why these steps are crucial:

Notarization: Having documents notarized confirms the identity of the signatories and adds a layer of protection against fraud. A notary public witnesses the signing of the document and affixes a seal to verify its authenticity. Notarization is often required for deeds, transfer forms, and other critical legal documents.

Recordation: Recording documents, such as deeds and business agreements, with the appropriate government office ensures that the transfers are a matter of public record. This public record provides legal evidence of the transfer and helps prevent disputes over ownership. For real estate, recording the deed with the county recorder's office is essential to validate the transfer and update property records.

Maintaining Proof of Transfers

Keeping thorough records of all asset transfers is essential for the smooth administration of your trust. Proper documentation provides clear evidence of the trust's ownership and helps prevent legal challenges. Here are some tips for maintaining proof of transfers:

Create a Master File: Maintain a master file that contains copies of all documents related to the trust. This file should include the trust agreement, deeds, assignment of ownership documents, transfer forms, account statements, and any correspondence with financial institutions or government agencies.

Organize by Asset Type: Organize documents by asset type for easy reference. For example, create separate sections for real estate, financial accounts, personal property, business interests, and intellectual property. This organization helps ensure that all documents are easily accessible when needed.

Keep Digital Copies: In addition to physical copies, keep digital copies of all documents. Use a secure digital storage solution, such as a cloud service with encryption, to protect sensitive information. Digital copies provide a backup in case physical documents are lost or damaged.

Regular Updates: Regularly update your records to reflect any new assets added to the trust or changes in your financial situation. Periodic reviews help ensure that all transfers are accurately documented and that the trust remains fully funded.

Communicate with Trustees: Ensure that the trustee and any successor trustees are aware of the location and organization of these documents. Providing clear instructions and access to these records helps facilitate smooth trust administration and asset management.

By completing the necessary forms, notarizing and recording documents, and maintaining thorough records, you can protect your assets and ensure they are managed and distributed according to your wishes. Properly documenting the transfer of assets into your living trust is a critical step in ensuring the trust's effectiveness and legal validity.

3.3 Common Mistakes to Avoid

Funding a living trust involves several critical steps, and making errors during this process can undermine the effectiveness of your trust. This section highlights common mistakes to avoid, ensuring that your trust operates smoothly and according to your wishes.

Failure to Transfer Assets Properly

One of the most significant mistakes in funding a living trust is failing to transfer assets correctly. If assets are not properly transferred, they may not be managed or distributed according to the terms of the trust.

Incomplete Transfers: Ensure that all steps in the transfer process are completed. For real estate, this means not only drafting and signing the deed but also recording it with the county recorder's office. For financial accounts, it means ensuring that the account titles are updated to reflect the trust's ownership.

Neglecting Personal Property: Personal property such as vehicles, jewellery, and collectibles should be formally transferred to the trust using a written assignment of ownership. Skipping this step can leave these assets outside the trust.

Overlooking Digital Assets: In today's digital age, it's essential to include digital assets such as online accounts, digital currencies, and intellectual property. Ensure these are also transferred into the trust where applicable.

Overlooking Certain Asset Types

Different types of assets require different procedures for transfer. Overlooking these differences can result in assets not being properly included in the trust.

Real Estate: Beyond residential properties, remember to include vacation homes, rental properties, and undeveloped land. Each property requires a separate deed transfer and recording.

Retirement Accounts: While you generally cannot transfer ownership of retirement accounts (e.g., IRAs and 401(k)s) to a trust during your lifetime without significant tax consequences, you can name the trust as the beneficiary. This ensures that the assets will eventually be managed by the trust.

Life Insurance Policies: Ensure that the trust is named as the beneficiary of your life insurance policies. This allows the policy proceeds to be managed according to the trust's terms.

Business Interests: If you have ownership in a business, particularly if it's a closely held corporation, partnership, or LLC, ensure the ownership interest is transferred to the trust. This might involve updating stock certificates, partnership agreements, or operating agreements.

Misunderstanding Tax Implications

Taxes can significantly impact the management and distribution of your trust assets. Misunderstanding these implications can lead to unintended tax consequences.

Estate Taxes: While assets in a living trust are subject to estate taxes, proper planning can help minimize these taxes. Work with a tax advisor to understand how best to structure your trust to minimize tax liability.

Income Taxes: The trust will have its own tax identification number and will need to file its own income tax returns if it generates income. Ensure that the trustee is aware of these responsibilities and is prepared to manage them.

Gift Taxes: Transferring assets to a trust is not typically subject to gift taxes, but large transfers might require reporting to the IRS. Consult with a tax professional to ensure compliance.

Ignoring State-Specific Laws

Trust laws vary significantly from state to state. Ignoring these differences can lead to problems with the legality and enforceability of your trust.

Recording Requirements: Some states have specific requirements for recording deeds and other documents. Ensure you comply with local requirements to validate property transfers.

Trustee Regulations: States have different rules regarding who can serve as a trustee and what powers they have. Make sure your choice of trustee complies with your state's regulations.

State Taxes: Some states have their own estate or inheritance taxes, which can affect how your trust is managed and distributed. Be aware of your state's tax laws and plan accordingly.

Failing to Update the Trust

Life circumstances change, and your trust should be updated to reflect these changes. Failing to update your trust can result in it not accurately reflecting your current wishes or financial situation.

Life Events: Major life events such as marriage, divorce, the birth of a child, or the death of a beneficiary should prompt an immediate review and update of your trust.

Acquiring New Assets: Any new assets acquired after the trust is created should be promptly transferred to the trust. This includes new real estate, financial accounts, and valuable personal property.

Changes in the Law: Tax laws and estate planning regulations change over time. Regular reviews with an estate planning attorney can ensure your trust remains compliant and optimized for current laws.

Not Communicating with Trustees and Beneficiaries

Lack of communication can lead to misunderstandings and disputes among trustees and beneficiaries.

Clear Instructions: Provide your trustee with clear instructions on managing and distributing the trust assets. This includes detailed information about your wishes and any specific conditions or terms.

Informing Beneficiaries: While it's not always necessary to share every detail, informing beneficiaries about the trust's existence and general terms can help manage their expectations and reduce potential conflicts.

Regular Updates: Keep open lines of communication with both the trustee and beneficiaries, especially when significant changes are made to the trust. Regular updates help ensure everyone is on the same page.

By being aware of these common mistakes and taking steps to avoid them, you can ensure that your living trust is properly funded and managed. This careful attention to detail helps protect your assets and ensures that your estate is administered according to your wishes.

Chapter 4: Trust Administration

Creating a living trust is only the first step in effective estate planning. Proper administration of the trust is crucial to ensure that your assets are managed and distributed according to your wishes. This chapter will cover the responsibilities of the trustee, the importance of periodic reviews and updates, and strategies for managing trust assets during the grantor's lifetime. Understanding these aspects of trust administration will help you maintain the integrity and effectiveness of your trust.

Responsibilities of the Trustee

The trustee plays a central role in the administration of a living trust. This individual or institution is responsible for managing the trust's assets and ensuring that the terms of the trust are carried out. Here are the primary responsibilities of a trustee:

Fiduciary Duty: The trustee has a fiduciary duty to act in the best interests of the beneficiaries. This duty requires the trustee to manage the trust's assets prudently and to avoid conflicts of interest. The trustee must always act with honesty and integrity.

Asset Management: The trustee is responsible for managing the trust's assets. This includes investing assets, collecting income, paying bills, and maintaining records. The trustee must make decisions that preserve and enhance the value of the trust's assets.

Record-Keeping: Accurate and detailed record-keeping is essential. The trustee must maintain records of all transactions, including receipts, disbursements, and investment performance. These records are crucial for tax reporting and for providing transparency to the beneficiaries.

Tax Responsibilities: The trustee must file the necessary tax returns for the trust. This includes federal and state income tax returns and, if applicable, estate tax returns. Proper tax management helps ensure compliance with tax laws and minimizes the tax burden on the trust.

Communication with Beneficiaries: The trustee must keep the beneficiaries informed about the trust's status and any significant decisions. Regular communication helps build trust and reduces the likelihood of disputes.

Distribution of Assets: The trustee is responsible for distributing the trust's assets to the beneficiaries according to the terms of the trust. This may involve making periodic distributions or distributing the assets upon the grantor's death.

Periodic Reviews and Updates

Regular reviews and updates are vital to maintaining the effectiveness of your living trust. Changes in your personal circumstances, financial situation, or the law may necessitate updates to the trust.

Annual Reviews: Conduct an annual review of your trust to ensure that it continues to meet your needs and reflects your current wishes. During this review, verify that all assets are properly titled in the name of the trust and update the list of assets as necessary.

Life Events: Significant life events such as marriage, divorce, the birth of a child, or the death of a beneficiary should prompt an immediate review and update of your trust. These events can have a profound impact on your estate plan and may require changes to the terms of the trust or the designation of beneficiaries.

Changes in Financial Situation: Major changes in your financial situation, such as acquiring new assets, selling property, or changes in income, should be reflected in your trust. Ensure that new assets are transferred to the trust and that any changes are documented.

Legal and Tax Changes: Stay informed about changes in the law that could affect your trust. Tax laws and estate planning regulations can change, and it's important to ensure that your trust remains compliant. Consult with an estate planning attorney periodically to review any legal changes that may impact your trust.

Updating Beneficiaries: Regularly review and update the list of beneficiaries to reflect your current wishes. This is especially important if your relationships with potential beneficiaries change over time.

Managing Assets During the Grantor's Lifetime

Effective management of trust assets during the grantor's lifetime is crucial for maintaining the trust's integrity and ensuring it meets its intended purpose.

Investment Strategy: Develop a sound investment strategy for the trust's assets. This strategy should balance growth with risk management to preserve the value of the trust while generating income. The trustee should regularly review and adjust the investment strategy based on changes in the market and the needs of the beneficiaries.

Income Generation: Ensure that the trust's assets are generating sufficient income to meet its obligations. This may include paying for the grantor's living expenses, funding distributions to beneficiaries, or covering administrative costs.

Expense Management: Keep trust expenses under control by carefully managing administrative costs, investment fees, and other expenses. Reducing unnecessary costs helps preserve the value of the trust's assets for the beneficiaries.

Healthcare and Support: If the trust is intended to provide for the grantor's healthcare and support, ensure that there are sufficient funds available to cover these expenses. This may include paying for medical bills, long-term care, or other support services.

Emergency Planning: Establish a plan for handling emergencies or unexpected events. This could include setting aside a reserve fund within the trust to cover unforeseen expenses or having a strategy in place for quickly liquidating assets if necessary.

Transition to Successor Trustee

Planning for the transition to a successor trustee is an important aspect of trust administration. This ensures that the trust continues to be managed effectively if the original trustee can no longer serve.

Clear Instructions: Provide clear instructions for the transition process in the trust document. Specify under what circumstances the successor trustee should take over and outline the steps for a smooth transition.

Successor Trustee Training: If possible, involve the successor trustee in the administration of the trust before they need to take over. This can include familiarizing them with the trust's assets, investment strategies, and the needs of the beneficiaries.

Notification of Beneficiaries: Inform the beneficiaries of the transition and provide them with contact information for the successor trustee. Clear communication helps ensure a smooth transition and reassures beneficiaries that their interests will continue to be protected.

Legal Compliance: Ensure that the transition complies with all legal requirements. This may involve updating documents, notifying financial institutions, and recording any changes with the relevant authorities.

By understanding and fulfilling these responsibilities, the trustee can effectively manage the trust, ensuring that it operates smoothly and meets the needs of the beneficiaries. Proper trust administration protects your assets, fulfils your wishes, and provides for your loved ones according to your estate plan.

In the next chapter, we will explore the process of updating the living trust. This includes making necessary modifications based on personal changes, the role of attorneys and financial advisors, and ensuring that the trust remains current and compliant with legal requirements.

4.1 Trustee's Responsibilities

The role of a trustee is fundamental to the successful administration of a living trust. The trustee is charged with managing the trust's assets in accordance with the grantor's wishes and ensuring that the beneficiaries receive their designated shares. This section delves into the various responsibilities of a trustee, highlighting the skills and diligence required to fulfil this role effectively.

Fiduciary Duty

A trustee's primary responsibility is to act as a fiduciary, which means they must act in the best interests of the trust and its beneficiaries. This duty encompasses several key obligations:

Loyalty: The trustee must prioritize the interests of the beneficiaries over their own. They cannot use the trust's assets for personal gain and must avoid conflicts of interest.

Impartiality: When there are multiple beneficiaries, the trustee must treat all beneficiaries fairly and impartially. This means balancing the needs and interests of current beneficiaries with those of future beneficiaries.

Care and Skill: The trustee must manage the trust's assets with a level of care and skill that a prudent person would use. This includes making informed and thoughtful decisions about investments and distributions.

Asset Management

Effective asset management is crucial to preserving and enhancing the value of the trust's assets. The trustee's duties in this area include:

Investment Decisions: The trustee is responsible for investing the trust's assets wisely. This involves developing a diversified investment strategy that balances risk and return, taking into account the trust's goals and the beneficiaries' needs.

Record-Keeping: Maintaining accurate and detailed records of all transactions is essential. This includes documenting income received, expenses paid, and changes in asset values. Good record-keeping ensures transparency and facilitates effective trust management.

Income Collection: The trustee must ensure that all income generated by the trust's assets is collected promptly. This may include rental income from real estate, dividends from stocks, and interest from bonds.

Expense Management: The trustee is responsible for paying the trust's expenses, which may include taxes, insurance premiums, maintenance costs, and professional fees. Managing these expenses carefully helps preserve the trust's assets.

Communication with Beneficiaries

Clear and regular communication with the beneficiaries is a critical aspect of a trustee's duties. This involves:

Providing Information: Beneficiaries have the right to be informed about the trust's administration and the status of the trust's assets. The trustee should provide regular reports and be transparent about their management decisions.

Responding to Inquiries: The trustee should be responsive to beneficiaries' questions and concerns. Addressing inquiries promptly and thoroughly helps build trust and prevent misunderstandings.

Distributing Assets: The trustee must distribute the trust's assets to the beneficiaries according to the terms set forth in the trust document. This includes making periodic distributions if specified and ensuring that the final distribution is handled correctly.

Tax Responsibilities

Managing the trust's tax obligations is another critical responsibility of the trustee. This includes:

Filing Tax Returns: The trustee must file federal and state income tax returns for the trust. This involves keeping track of the trust's income and expenses and ensuring that all tax obligations are met on time.

Paying Taxes: The trustee is responsible for paying any taxes owed by the trust. This may include income taxes, property taxes, and, if applicable, estate taxes.

Tax Planning: Effective tax planning can help minimize the trust's tax liabilities. The trustee should work with tax professionals to develop strategies that optimize the trust's tax position, such as timing distributions to take advantage of lower tax rates.

Compliance with Legal Requirements

The trustee must ensure that the trust complies with all applicable laws and regulations. This involves:

Understanding State Laws: Trust laws vary by state, so the trustee must be familiar with the legal requirements in the state where the trust is administered. This includes understanding the duties and powers of a trustee, as well as any specific requirements for reporting and record-keeping.

Updating Legal Documents: As laws and circumstances change, the trustee may need to update the trust's legal documents. This could involve amending the trust document, updating deeds for real estate, or revising beneficiary designations.

Consulting with Professionals: The trustee should consult with legal, financial, and tax professionals to ensure that they are fulfilling their duties correctly and that the trust is compliant with all relevant laws.

Managing Distributions

The trustee is responsible for distributing the trust's assets according to the terms set forth in the trust document. This includes:

Interpreting the Trust Document: The trustee must carefully interpret the trust document to understand the grantor's intentions and ensure that distributions are made correctly. This includes understanding any conditions or restrictions on distributions.

Making Distributions: The trustee must ensure that distributions are made in a timely and accurate manner. This may involve making periodic distributions to beneficiaries or distributing assets upon the grantor's death.

Documenting Distributions: The trustee should keep detailed records of all distributions, including the amounts distributed, the recipients, and the dates. This documentation helps ensure transparency and accountability.

By understanding and fulfilling these responsibilities, the trustee can effectively manage the trust, ensuring that it operates smoothly and meets the needs of the beneficiaries. Proper trust administration protects your assets, fulfils your wishes, and provides for your loved ones according to your estate plan.

4.2 Periodic Reviews and Updates

Regular reviews and updates of your living trust are essential to ensure it remains effective and reflective of your current wishes and circumstances. Changes in your personal life, financial situation, or the legal landscape can all necessitate adjustments to your trust. This section outlines the importance of periodic reviews and provides a guide on how to conduct them effectively.

Importance of Regular Reviews

Regular reviews of your living trust are crucial for several reasons:

Reflecting Life Changes: Significant life events, such as marriage, divorce, the birth of a child, or the death of a beneficiary, can impact your estate planning needs. Regular reviews ensure that your trust accurately reflects these changes.

Updating Financial Information: Your financial situation can change over time due to asset acquisition, changes in income, or fluctuations in the value of your investments. Regular updates ensure that all your assets are included in the trust and that their current values are accurately reflected.

Ensuring Legal Compliance: Tax laws and estate planning regulations are subject to change. Regular reviews help ensure that your trust remains compliant with current laws and takes advantage of any new legal benefits.

Maintaining Clear Instructions: Over time, your intentions for the distribution of your assets may evolve. Periodic updates ensure that your instructions remain clear and that the trustee can effectively carry out your wishes.

Conducting an Annual Review

An annual review is a recommended practice for keeping your living trust up to date. Here's a step-by-step guide to conducting an effective annual review:

Review Asset Inventory: Start by reviewing the inventory of assets listed in your trust. Ensure that all new assets acquired over the past year are included and that any assets you no longer own are removed. Verify the current values of your assets and update this information as needed.

Evaluate Beneficiary Designations: Examine the list of beneficiaries to ensure it reflects your current wishes. If there have been changes in your relationships or if new potential beneficiaries have emerged, update the designations accordingly

Assess Trustee Performance: Evaluate the performance of your current trustee. Ensure they are fulfilling their duties effectively and that there are no conflicts of interest. If necessary, consider appointing a new trustee or successor trustees to ensure continued effective management of the trust.

Update Legal Documents: Review the legal language in your trust document. Ensure that all provisions are still relevant and that any changes in the law are reflected. This may require consultation with an estate planning attorney to ensure compliance with current legal standards.

Check Tax Implications: Consult with a tax advisor to review the tax implications of your trust. Ensure that your trust is structured in a way that minimizes tax liabilities and takes advantage of any new tax laws or strategies.

Responding to Life Events

In addition to annual reviews, you should update your living trust in response to significant life events. Here are some common life events that warrant an immediate review and update:

Marriage or Divorce: Changes in marital status can significantly impact your estate plan. Update your trust to reflect any changes in beneficiary designations and to ensure that your spouse or ex-spouse is included or excluded as desired.

Birth or Adoption of a Child: The addition of a new child to your family should prompt an update to your trust. Ensure that provisions are made for the new child's financial security and that any necessary guardianship arrangements are included.

Death of a Beneficiary or Trustee: The death of a named beneficiary or trustee requires an immediate update to your trust. Designate new beneficiaries or trustees as needed and update the distribution plan accordingly.

Significant Changes in Financial Situation: Major changes in your financial situation, such as acquiring or selling a business, receiving a large inheritance, or experiencing significant investment gains or losses, should be reflected in your trust.

Relocation to a New State: Moving to a new state can affect your estate plan due to differences in state laws. Review and update your trust to ensure compliance with the laws of your new state of residence.

Legal and Tax Considerations

Staying informed about changes in the legal and tax landscape is crucial for maintaining an effective living trust. Here are some steps to ensure your trust remains compliant and optimized:

Consult with Professionals: Regularly consult with an estate planning attorney and a tax advisor to stay updated on changes in laws and regulations. These professionals can provide guidance on how to adjust your trust to take advantage of new legal benefits and minimize tax liabilities.

Attend Educational Seminars: Participate in estate planning seminars and workshops to stay informed about best practices and new developments in the field. This knowledge can help you make informed decisions about your trust.

Monitor Legislative Changes: Keep an eye on changes in estate planning and tax laws at both the federal and state levels. This can include subscribing to newsletters, joining estate planning associations, or following relevant news sources.

Implement Legal Updates: When significant legal changes occur, update your trust document to reflect these changes. This may involve adding new clauses, revising existing provisions, or restructuring the trust entirely.

Maintaining Flexibility

One of the key benefits of a living trust is its flexibility. Ensure that your trust document includes provisions that allow for future modifications. Here are some strategies to maintain flexibility:

Include Amendment Provisions: Clearly outline the process for amending the trust document. This ensures that you can make changes as needed without complications.

Appoint a Trust Protector: Consider appointing a trust protector—a person or entity with the authority to make certain changes to the trust if circumstances change. This can provide an additional layer of flexibility and oversight.

Regular Communication with Beneficiaries: Maintain open lines of communication with your beneficiaries. Understanding their needs and circumstances can help you make informed decisions about updates to the trust.

By conducting regular reviews and updates, you can ensure that your living trust remains a dynamic and effective tool for managing your estate. Keeping the trust current with your wishes, financial situation, and legal requirements will help protect your assets and provide for your loved ones according to your intentions.

4.3 Managing Trust Assets During the Grantor's Lifetime

Managing trust assets effectively during the grantor's lifetime is crucial to maintaining the trust's integrity and ensuring it meets its intended purpose. This involves developing strategies for investment, generating income, controlling expenses, and planning for healthcare and emergencies. Proper management of these aspects ensures that the trust operates smoothly and supports the grantors and beneficiaries' needs.

Investment Strategies

An effective investment strategy is key to preserving and growing the trust's assets. Here are some considerations for developing a sound investment approach:

Risk Assessment: Assess the level of risk that is appropriate for the trust's assets. This assessment should consider the grantor's financial goals, the beneficiaries' needs, and the time horizon for distributing the assets.

Diversification: Diversify the trust's investment portfolio to reduce risk and enhance returns. This can involve investing in a mix of asset classes such as stocks, bonds, real estate, and alternative investments. Diversification helps protect the trust's assets from market volatility.

Regular Monitoring: Monitor the performance of the trust's investments regularly. This includes reviewing financial statements, analysing market trends, and adjusting the investment strategy as needed to respond to changing conditions.

Professional Advice: Consider working with a financial advisor or investment manager to develop and implement an investment strategy. These professionals can provide expertise and guidance to optimize the trust's portfolio.

Income Generation

Generating sufficient income from the trust's assets is essential to meet its obligations and support the grantor and beneficiaries. Here are strategies for maximizing income:

Interest and Dividends: Invest in income-producing assets such as bonds and dividend-paying stocks. These assets provide regular income that can be used to cover expenses and fund distributions.

Rental Income: If the trust owns real estate, consider renting out properties to generate rental income. This income can help offset the costs of maintaining the properties and contribute to the trust's overall cash flow.

Royalties and Licensing: If the trust holds intellectual property, explore opportunities to generate income through royalties and licensing agreements. This can include licensing patents, trademarks, or copyrights to third parties.

Business Income: If the trust owns a business or business interests, ensure that the business is managed effectively to generate profits. This may involve appointing a professional manager or actively overseeing the business operations.

Expense Management

Controlling expenses is critical to preserving the trust's assets and ensuring that funds are available for the grantors and beneficiaries' needs. Here are some tips for effective expense management:

Budgeting: Develop a budget for the trust's expenses, including administrative costs, taxes, insurance, and maintenance. A well-planned budget helps ensure that expenses are controlled, and funds are allocated efficiently.

Cost Reduction: Identify opportunities to reduce costs without compromising the trust's objectives. This can include negotiating lower fees with service providers, consolidating accounts to reduce administrative costs, and implementing energy-saving measures for real estate holdings.

Regular Audits: Conduct regular audits of the trust's expenses to identify any areas of overspending or inefficiency. Audits help ensure accountability and transparency in the trust's financial management.

Professional Assistance: Consider engaging professionals such as accountants or estate planners to provide advice on managing expenses. These experts can offer insights into cost-saving strategies and help ensure compliance with legal and tax obligations.

Healthcare and Support

If the trust is intended to provide for the grantor's healthcare and support, ensure that there are sufficient funds available to cover these expenses. Here's how to plan for healthcare and support:

Healthcare Coverage: Ensure that the grantor has adequate healthcare coverage, including medical, dental, and vision insurance. Review the coverage regularly to ensure it meets the grantor's needs and adjust as necessary.

Long-Term Care Planning: Consider the potential need for long-term care and explore options for funding these costs. This may involve purchasing long-term care insurance, setting aside a reserve fund, or exploring government programs and benefits.

Support Services: Plan for the grantor's support needs, such as in-home care, assisted living, or transportation services. Ensure that funds are available to cover these services and that arrangements are in place to provide timely support.

Emergency Preparedness: Establish a plan for handling emergencies or unexpected healthcare needs. This could include setting aside a reserve fund within the trust to cover unforeseen expenses or having a strategy in place for quickly accessing funds if necessary.

Planning for Emergencies

Having a plan in place for emergencies or unexpected events is crucial for maintaining the trust's stability and ensuring that the grantors and beneficiaries' needs are met. Here are some strategies for emergency planning:

Emergency Fund: Set aside a portion of the trust's assets as an emergency fund. This fund can be used to cover unexpected expenses such as medical emergencies, legal fees, or urgent property repairs.

Access to Liquid Assets: Ensure that the trust has access to liquid assets that can be quickly converted to cash if needed. This may involve maintaining a portion of the trust's portfolio in cash or cash equivalents such as money market funds.

Disaster Preparedness: Develop a disaster preparedness plan that outlines steps to take in the event of a natural disaster or other emergencies. This plan should include procedures for protecting the trust's assets and ensuring the safety and well-being of the grantor and beneficiaries.

Regular Reviews: Periodically review the emergency plan to ensure it remains relevant and effective. Update the plan as needed to address changes in circumstances or new risks.

By effectively managing the trust's assets during the grantor's lifetime, you can ensure that the trust operates smoothly and meets its intended purpose. Proper management helps protect the trust's assets, support the grantor's needs, and provide for the beneficiaries according to your estate plan.

Chapter 5: Updating and Modifying the Trust

As life circumstances and financial situations evolve, it is essential to update and modify your living trust to ensure it remains aligned with your current goals and intentions. Regularly reviewing and making necessary changes to your trust can help avoid potential conflicts, ensure legal compliance, and maintain the effectiveness of your estate plan. This chapter explores the reasons for modifying a trust, the process involved, and the role of legal and financial advisors in guiding these updates.

Reasons for Modifying a Trust

Several events and circumstances may prompt you to modify your living trust. Here are some common reasons for making updates:

Life Events: Significant life changes, such as marriage, divorce, the birth or adoption of a child, or the death of a loved one, may necessitate updates to your trust. These events can impact your estate planning goals and may require changes to beneficiary designations or distribution plans.

Changes in Financial Situation: Major changes in your financial situation, such as acquiring new assets, selling property, or experiencing a significant increase or decrease in wealth, should be reflected in your trust. Ensuring that all assets are properly included and titled in the trust is essential for maintaining an accurate and effective estate plan.

Tax Law Changes: Changes in tax laws and regulations can affect your estate planning strategy. Modifying your trust to reflect these changes can help optimize tax benefits and minimize liabilities for your estate and beneficiaries.

Beneficiary Updates: Changes in relationships with beneficiaries, such as estrangement or reconciliation, may prompt updates to the trust. It is important to regularly review beneficiary designations to ensure they reflect your current wishes and circumstances.

Trustee Changes: If your trustee or successor trustee is unable or unwilling to serve, or if you have concerns about their ability to fulfil their duties, it may be necessary to appoint a new trustee. This ensures that the trust is managed effectively and in accordance with your intentions.

Legal or Regulatory Changes: Changes in state or federal laws, or shifts in the legal landscape, may necessitate updates to your trust to ensure compliance and to take advantage of new legal opportunities.

Process for Modifying a Trust

Updating a living trust involves a series of steps to ensure that modifications are legally valid and enforceable. Here's a guide to the modification process:

Review the Trust Document: Start by reviewing the current trust document to identify the specific provisions that need to be updated or amended. Make a list of the changes you want to make and consider how these changes align with your overall estate planning goals.

Consult with Professionals: Work with an estate planning attorney to discuss your desired changes and ensure that they are drafted correctly. An attorney can provide guidance on legal requirements, potential tax implications, and strategies for implementing your updates effectively.

Draft the Amendment: Draft a trust amendment that clearly outlines the changes you wish to make. This document should include the specific sections of the trust being modified, the new terms or provisions, and the reasons for the changes.

Execute the Amendment: Sign the amendment in the presence of a notary public and any required witnesses. The notarization and witnessing add a layer of legal validity to the document and help prevent challenges to its authenticity.

Distribute the Amendment: Provide copies of the amendment to your trustee, successor trustees, and any other relevant parties. Ensure that all parties involved in the administration of the trust are aware of the changes and have access to the updated document.

Update Related Documents: Review and update any related estate planning documents, such as wills, powers of attorney, and beneficiary designations, to ensure consistency with the modified trust.

Role of Legal and Financial Advisors

Legal and financial advisors play a crucial role in guiding the trust modification process. Here's how they can assist:

Legal Expertise: An estate planning attorney can ensure that your trust modifications comply with state and federal laws. They can help draft clear and legally sound amendments, provide insights into potential legal risks, and offer solutions to complex estate planning challenges.

Tax Planning: A tax advisor can assess the tax implications of your proposed changes and help you optimize your estate plan for tax efficiency. They can provide strategies to minimize estate and income taxes and ensure compliance with current tax laws.

Financial Guidance: A financial advisor can help you assess the impact of trust modifications on your overall financial plan. They can assist with investment strategies, cash flow management, and long-term financial planning to support your estate planning goals.

Regular Reviews: Advisors can facilitate regular reviews of your trust and estate plan, helping you stay informed about changes in the legal and financial landscape and making proactive recommendations for updates.

Conflict Resolution: In the event of disputes or conflicts among beneficiaries, advisors can provide mediation and conflict resolution services. Their expertise can help facilitate discussions and reach mutually agreeable solutions.

Maintaining Flexibility

Maintaining flexibility in your trust is essential for adapting to changing circumstances and ensuring that your estate plan remains relevant and effective. Here are some strategies for maintaining flexibility:

Include Amendment Provisions: Clearly outline the process for amending the trust in the trust document. This ensures that you can make changes as needed without complications.

Use Trust Protectors: Consider appointing a trust protector—a person or entity with the authority to make certain changes to the trust if circumstances change. This provides an additional layer of flexibility and oversight.

Regular Communication: Maintain open lines of communication with your trustee, beneficiaries, and advisors. Understanding their needs and circumstances can help you make informed decisions about updates to the trust.

By regularly reviewing and updating your living trust, you can ensure that it remains a dynamic and effective tool for managing your estate. Keeping the trust current with your wishes, financial situation, and legal requirements will help protect your assets and provide for your loved ones according to your intentions.

5.1 Reasons for Modifying a Trust

Modifying a living trust is a critical aspect of maintaining its relevance and effectiveness as an estate planning tool. Life is full of changes, and your trust should reflect those changes to ensure that your assets are protected and distributed according to your current wishes. This section explores the various reasons that may necessitate modifications to your trust and highlights the importance of keeping it up to date.

Life Events

Significant life events can have a profound impact on your estate planning needs and may require adjustments to your trust. Here are some common life events that warrant updates:

Marriage or Divorce: Changes in marital status can significantly affect your estate plan. If you marry, you may want to include your new spouse as a beneficiary or trustee. Conversely, if you divorce, you may wish to remove your ex-spouse from the trust to prevent them from receiving any benefits.

Birth or Adoption of a Child: The arrival of a new child or the adoption of a child is a significant life event that should be reflected in your trust. You may want to add provisions for their financial security, such as designating them as a beneficiary or setting up a sub-trust to provide for their education and other needs.

Death of a Beneficiary or Trustee: The death of a named beneficiary or trustee requires immediate updates to your trust. You may need to redistribute assets to other beneficiaries or appoint a new trustee to ensure the trust is managed effectively.

Changes in Relationships: Relationships with family members and friends can change over time, impacting your decisions regarding beneficiaries and trustees. If you become estranged from a beneficiary or reconcile with someone previously excluded, you may need to update the trust to reflect these changes.

Changes in Financial Situation

Your financial situation can change due to various factors, such as acquiring new assets, selling property, or experiencing significant financial growth or decline. Here's how these changes may impact your trust:

Asset Acquisition: When you acquire new assets, such as real estate, investments, or valuable personal property, it is crucial to transfer ownership of these assets into the trust. This ensures they are protected and managed according to the terms of the trust.

Asset Disposition: If you sell or dispose of assets, update your trust to reflect these changes. Removing assets that are no longer part of your estate helps maintain an accurate and effective estate plan.

Changes in Wealth: Significant increases or decreases in wealth may necessitate adjustments to your distribution plans. For example, you may want to provide additional support to beneficiaries or create charitable provisions if your financial situation improves.

Tax Law Changes

Tax laws and regulations are subject to change, and these changes can have a substantial impact on your estate planning strategy. Here's why keeping your trust updated in response to tax law changes is essential:

Estate Tax Thresholds: Changes in estate tax thresholds can affect the tax liability of your estate. If the exemption amount increases, you may have more flexibility in distributing your assets without incurring taxes. Conversely, if the exemption decreases, you may need to revise your plan to minimize tax liabilities.

Income Tax Implications: Changes in income tax laws can affect the taxation of trust income. Updating your trust to take advantage of favourable tax treatments or to mitigate new tax burdens can help optimize your estate plan.

Gift Tax Considerations: Modifications to gift tax rules can impact your ability to transfer assets during your lifetime. Keeping your trust updated considering these changes can help you make informed decisions about gifting strategies.

Beneficiary Updates

Regularly reviewing and updating beneficiary designations is crucial for ensuring that your trust aligns with your current intentions. Here's why beneficiary updates are important:

Changing Needs: Beneficiaries' needs and circumstances can change over time. For example, a beneficiary may face financial difficulties or health challenges that require additional support. Updating your trust to provide for these needs can ensure that your estate plan remains relevant and effective.

Adding or Removing Beneficiaries: As your relationships evolve, you may wish to add new beneficiaries or remove existing ones. For instance, you might want to include a grandchild born after the trust was created or remove a beneficiary with whom you have lost contact.

Equalizing Inheritances: If you wish to equalize inheritances among beneficiaries, updating your trust can help achieve this goal. This may involve adjusting distribution percentages or creating specific provisions for individual beneficiaries.

Trustee Changes

The selection of a trustee is a critical decision in estate planning, and changes may be necessary over time. Here are some reasons for updating trustee designations:

Inability to Serve: A trustee may become unable or unwilling to serve due to health issues, relocation, or other personal circumstances. In such cases, appointing a new trustee ensures that the trust continues to be managed effectively.

Performance Concerns: If you have concerns about a trustee's performance or ability to fulfill their duties, consider appointing a new trustee who can better manage the trust assets and carry out your intentions.

Successor Trustees: As time passes, the designated successor trustees may need to be updated. Ensuring that there are qualified and willing individuals to step into the trustee role is essential for maintaining the trust's integrity.

Legal or Regulatory Changes

Changes in the legal landscape can necessitate updates to your trust to ensure compliance and take advantage of new legal opportunities:

State Law Variations: If you move to a new state, your trust may need to be updated to comply with that state's laws. Differences in trust law, tax regulations, and probate procedures can impact your estate plan.

New Legislation: Legislative changes can introduce new opportunities or requirements for estate planning. Staying informed about these changes and updating your trust accordingly can help optimize your plan and protect your assets.

Court Rulings: Legal precedents set by court rulings can affect trust administration and interpretation. Consulting with an estate planning attorney to understand these implications and make necessary updates is essential.

By understanding the reasons for modifying a trust and proactively addressing these changes, you can ensure that your living trust remains a flexible and effective tool for managing your estate. Regular updates help protect your assets, provide for your loved ones, and reflect your current wishes and circumstances.

5.2 Process for Modifying a Trust

Modifying a living trust is an essential part of keeping your estate plan current and effective. This process involves adjusting reflect changes in your life, finances, or the law. To ensure the modifications are legally valid and enforceable, it's important to follow a structured approach. Here's a detailed guide on the process for modifying a trust.

Review the Trust Document

Before making any modifications, start by reviewing the existing trust document thoroughly. This review helps identify the specific provisions that need updating or amendment. Consider the following steps during this initial review:

Identify Outdated Provisions: Look for any provisions that no longer align with your current wishes or circumstances. This may include outdated beneficiary designations, trustee appointments, or distribution plans.

Note Legal or Tax Changes: Identify any sections that might be affected by recent changes in laws or tax regulations. Consider consulting with a legal expert to understand these impacts fully.

Evaluate Financial Implications: Assess whether the current asset allocations and financial strategies still meet your estate planning goals. Consider any recent changes in your financial situation that might necessitate updates.

Consult with Professionals

Working with estate planning professionals is crucial to ensure that your trust modifications are correctly executed and legally sound. Here's how they can assist:

Estate Planning Attorney: An attorney can provide guidance on legal requirements and help draft amendments or restatements of your trust. They ensure that your modifications comply with current laws and that the language used is precise and enforceable.

Tax Advisor: A tax advisor can evaluate the tax implications of your proposed changes and suggest strategies to minimize tax liabilities. They help you understand the potential impact on estate, gift, and income taxes.

Financial Advisor: A financial advisor can assess the broader implications of your trust modifications on your overall financial plan. They can offer insights into investment strategies, cash flow management, and other financial considerations.

Draft the Amendment

Once you've identified the necessary changes and consulted with professionals, draft a formal amendment to the trust document. Here's what to include:

Title and Date: Clearly title the document as an amendment and include the date of the amendment. Specify which sections of the original trust document are being amended.

Clear Language: Use clear and precise language to outline the specific changes you are making. This might include changes to beneficiary designations, trustee appointments, or asset distributions.

Rationale for Changes: Briefly explain the reasons for the modifications, especially if they are significant. This can provide context and clarity for future reference.

Reference the Original Trust: Reference the original trust document by its full name and date of execution to ensure continuity and legal clarity.

Execute the Amendment

To ensure the amendment is legally valid, follow these execution steps:

Sign the Amendment: The grantor must sign the amendment in the presence of a notary public. Notarization helps authenticate the document and reduces the risk of legal challenges.

Witness Signatures: Depending on state requirements, you may also need witnesses to sign the amendment. Having witnesses adds another layer of legal protection.

Notarization: A notary public must verify the signatures to provide an official seal. This step ensures the amendment's authenticity and legal standing.

Distribute the Amendment

After executing the amendment, distribute copies to relevant parties involved in the trust administration:

Trustee and Successor Trustees: Provide copies to the current trustee and any successor trustees. Ensure they are aware of the changes and understand their responsibilities under the modified trust.

Beneficiaries: Consider informing beneficiaries of the modifications, especially if they impact their interests or involve significant changes. Clear communication helps manage expectations and prevent disputes.

Professional Advisors: Share the updated trust document with your legal, tax, and financial advisors. Keeping them informed ensures that your entire estate planning team is aligned and can provide cohesive support.

Update Related Documents

Ensure that all related estate planning documents are consistent with the modified trust:

Will: Update your will to reflect any changes in asset distribution or beneficiary designations. This helps prevent conflicts between your will and trust.

Powers of Attorney: Review and update any powers of attorney to ensure they align with your current intentions and estate planning strategy.

Beneficiary Designations: Ensure that beneficiary designations on life insurance policies, retirement accounts, and other financial instruments are consistent with the trust modifications.

Consider Restating the Trust

If you have made numerous or significant amendments over time, consider restating the entire trust. A restatement involves rewriting the trust document in its entirety, incorporating all previous amendments and current changes into a single cohesive document. This approach can simplify the trust, making it easier to understand and administer.

Maintain Flexibility for Future Changes

Estate planning is a dynamic process, and maintaining flexibility in your trust is essential. Here are some strategies to keep your trust adaptable:

Include Amendment Provisions: Clearly outline the process for future amendments in the trust document. This ensures you can make changes as needed without complications.

Appoint a Trust Protector: Consider designating a trust protector who has the authority to make specific changes to the trust if circumstances change. This can provide an additional layer of oversight and adaptability.

Regular Reviews: Schedule regular reviews of your trust with your advisors to ensure it remains aligned with your goals and legal requirements. Regular updates help maintain the trust's effectiveness and relevance.

By following a structured process for modifying your living trust and working with experienced professionals, you can ensure that your estate plan remains current, effective, and reflective of your wishes. Regular updates help protect your assets and provide for your loved ones according to your intentions.

5.3 Role of Legal and Financial Advisor

Legal and financial advisors play an essential role in maintaining the effectiveness of your living trust. Their expertise ensures that your trust remains compliant with current laws and aligns with your financial goals. This section explores the specific roles of these professionals and highlights the benefits of involving them in your estate planning process.

Legal Advisors

An estate planning attorney is a critical component of your advisory team. Here's how they can assist with trust modifications:

Drafting and Reviewing Documents: An attorney can draft trust amendments or restatements and ensure that the language is precise and enforceable. They also review existing documents to identify any potential legal issues or inconsistencies.

Ensuring Legal Compliance: Trust laws vary by state, and an attorney ensures your trust complies with these laws. They stay updated on legislative changes and provide guidance on how these changes impact your estate plan.

Interpreting Legal Language: Attorneys help interpret complex legal language within the trust document, ensuring that you fully understand the implications of your decisions and any modifications.

Resolving Disputes: In the event of disputes among beneficiaries or between the trustee and beneficiaries, an attorney can provide mediation and legal counsel to resolve conflicts and protect your interests.

Protecting Privacy: Legal advisors ensure that your estate planning documents are handled with confidentiality, protecting your privacy and that of your beneficiaries.

Tax Advisors

Tax considerations are a critical aspect of estate planning. A tax advisor plays a crucial role in optimizing your trust for tax efficiency:

Minimizing Tax Liabilities: Tax advisors help structure your trust to minimize estate, gift, and income taxes. They provide strategies to reduce the tax burden on your estate and beneficiaries.

Navigating Tax Law Changes: Tax laws are subject to change, and a tax advisor stays informed about these changes to ensure your trust remains compliant and takes advantage of any new tax benefits.

Filing Tax Returns: A tax advisor assists the trustee in preparing and filing the necessary tax returns for the trust. This includes federal and state income tax returns, as well as any applicable estate tax filings.

Advising on Charitable Contributions: If your trust includes charitable contributions, a tax advisor can provide guidance on the tax implications and benefits of these gifts, ensuring that they are structured to maximize tax efficiency.

Analysing Distribution Strategies: Tax advisors help evaluate the tax impact of different distribution strategies, advising on the timing and structure of distributions to minimize taxes.

Financial Advisors

A financial advisor provides strategic insights into managing the trust's assets and aligning them with your long-term goals:

Investment Management: Financial advisors develop and implement investment strategies that align with the trust's objectives and the risk tolerance of the beneficiaries. They regularly review and adjust the portfolio to respond to market changes.

Cash Flow Planning: Advisors help ensure that the trust generates sufficient income to meet its obligations, such as funding distributions, covering administrative expenses, and supporting the grantor's needs.

Assessing Financial Goals: Financial advisors work with you to assess and refine your financial goals, ensuring that the trust's management aligns with these objectives. They provide guidance on balancing growth, income, and risk.

Advising on Asset Allocation: Advisors provide insights into optimal asset allocation within the trust, helping diversify the portfolio to reduce risk and enhance returns.

Long-Term Planning: Financial advisors assist with long-term financial planning, including retirement planning, education funding, and other financial goals, ensuring that your estate plan supports your overall financial strategy.

Benefits of an Integrated Advisory Team

Working with an integrated team of legal, tax, and financial advisors offers several benefits:

Holistic Planning: An integrated team provides a comprehensive approach to estate planning, ensuring that all aspects of your trust are considered and aligned with your goals.

Coordinated Strategies: Advisors collaborate to develop coordinated strategies that optimize the management of your trust, taking into account legal, tax, and financial considerations.

Proactive Risk Management: An advisory team identifies potential risks and develops strategies to mitigate them, protecting your assets and ensuring the effectiveness of your estate plan.

Efficient Implementation: Advisors work together to implement changes efficiently and accurately, minimizing the risk of errors or omissions.

Personalized Advice: An integrated team provides personalized advice tailored to your unique circumstances, ensuring that your trust reflects your specific needs and preferences.

Regular Reviews and Ongoing Communication

Regular reviews and ongoing communication with your advisory team are crucial for maintaining the effectiveness of your trust:

Annual Reviews: Schedule annual reviews with your advisors to assess the trust's performance and identify any necessary updates or adjustments.

Life Event Updates: Communicate promptly with your advisors about significant life events, such as marriage, divorce, birth, or death, to ensure that your trust is updated accordingly.

Monitoring Legislative Changes: Stay informed about changes in laws and regulations that may affect your trust, and work with your advisors to implement any necessary updates.

Transparent Communication: Maintain open and transparent communication with your advisors to ensure that your goals and intentions are clearly understood and reflected in your estate plan.

By engaging a team of legal, tax, and financial advisors, you can ensure that your living trust is effectively managed and remains aligned with your goals. Their expertise and guidance help navigate the complexities of estate planning, protect your assets, and provide for your loved ones according to your wishes.

Chapter 6: Revocable vs. Irrevocable Trusts

When establishing a trust as part of your estate planning, it's crucial to understand the differences between revocable and irrevocable trusts. Each type of trust offers unique benefits and limitations that can impact your estate plan and financial strategy. This chapter explores the characteristics, advantages, and disadvantages of revocable and irrevocable trusts, helping you make an informed decision that aligns with your goals.

Revocable Trusts

A revocable trust, also known as a living trust, is a flexible estate planning tool that allows the grantor to retain control over the trust assets during their lifetime. Here are some key features and benefits of revocable trusts:

Flexibility and Control: One of the main advantages of a revocable trust is its flexibility. The grantor can modify, amend, or revoke the trust at any time during their lifetime, allowing them to adapt the trust to changing circumstances or preferences. This control extends to the management and distribution of the trust assets, enabling the grantor to make decisions based on evolving needs and goals.

Avoiding Probate: A revocable trust can help your estate avoid probate, the legal process of distributing assets after death. By transferring assets into the trust, they are no longer part of your probate estate, reducing the time, expense, and complexity associated with the probate process. This can also help maintain privacy, as the trust assets and distributions are not subject to public record.

Incapacity Planning: A revocable trust provides a mechanism for managing your assets in the event of incapacity. By appointing a successor trustee, you can ensure that your financial affairs are handled according to your wishes if you become unable to manage them yourself. This can help avoid the need for a court-appointed guardianship or conservatorship, preserving your autonomy and reducing administrative burdens on your family.

Ongoing Management: Revocable trusts allow for seamless management of assets during the grantor's lifetime and after their death. The trustee can continue to manage and distribute assets according to the terms of the trust, providing continuity and stability for the beneficiaries.

Disadvantages of Revocable Trusts

While revocable trusts offer significant benefits, they also have some limitations:

No Asset Protection: Assets held in a revocable trust are not protected from creditors, lawsuits, or divorce settlements. Because the grantor retains control over the trust assets, they are considered part of the grantor's estate and subject to claims from creditors and legal judgments.

No Tax Benefits: Revocable trusts do not provide tax benefits or shelter assets from estate taxes. The trust's assets are still considered part of the grantor's taxable estate, and income generated by the trust is reported on the grantor's personal income tax return.

Costs and Complexity: Establishing and maintaining a revocable trust can involve legal and administrative costs. While the trust can simplify asset management, it also requires ongoing attention to ensure that assets are properly titled in the trust and that the trust document remains up to date.

Irrevocable Trusts

An irrevocable trust is a more rigid estate planning tool that involves transferring ownership of assets to the trust permanently. Once the trust is established, the grantor relinquishes control over the assets, and the trust cannot be amended or revoked without the consent of the beneficiaries. Here are some key features and benefits of irrevocable trusts:

Asset Protection: Irrevocable trusts provide robust asset protection, shielding the trust assets from creditors, lawsuits, and divorce settlements. Because the grantor no longer owns the assets, they are not considered part of the grantor's estate and are protected from personal liabilities.

Tax Benefits: Irrevocable trusts offer potential tax benefits, such as reducing estate and gift taxes. By transferring assets out of the grantor's estate, the trust can help minimize the taxable estate and reduce the potential tax burden on beneficiaries. Additionally, income generated by the trust is taxed at the trust's rate, which may be advantageous in certain circumstances.

Charitable Giving: Irrevocable trusts can facilitate charitable giving by allowing the grantor to establish a charitable trust or foundation. This can provide tax benefits while supporting causes that align with the grantor's values and philanthropic goals.

Estate Planning Goals: Irrevocable trusts can be tailored to achieve specific estate planning goals, such as preserving wealth for future generations, providing for special needs beneficiaries, or establishing a family legacy. The trust's terms can be customized to reflect the grantor's intentions and provide long-term benefits to beneficiaries.

Disadvantages of Irrevocable Trusts

Despite their advantages, irrevocable trusts also have some drawbacks:

Lack of Control: Once assets are transferred to an irrevocable trust, the grantor relinquishes control over them. This means that the grantor cannot easily change the terms of the trust or access the assets for personal use, which may be a significant limitation for those who value flexibility.

Complexity and Costs: Establishing an irrevocable trust can be complex and expensive, requiring legal and financial expertise to draft and administer the trust. The trust may also have ongoing administrative and tax filing requirements, adding to the complexity and cost.

Irrevocability: The permanence of an irrevocable trust can be a disadvantage if the grantor's circumstances or goals change. Once established, the trust cannot be easily modified or revoked, which may limit the grantor's ability to adapt the trust to changing needs.

Choosing the Right Trust for Your Needs

Deciding between a revocable and irrevocable trust depends on your specific estate planning goals, financial situation, and personal preferences. Here are some factors to consider when making your decision:

Goals and Objectives: Consider your primary goals for establishing a trust, such as asset protection, tax planning, or providing for beneficiaries. Determine which type of trust best aligns with these objectives.

Control and Flexibility: Assess your comfort level with relinquishing control over assets and the importance of flexibility in your estate plan. A revocable trust offers greater control, while an irrevocable trust provides more protection.

Legal and Tax Implications: Consult with legal and tax advisors to understand the implications of each type of trust and how they fit into your overall estate planning strategy. Advisors can provide guidance on the best trust structure for your needs and help you navigate the complexities of trust law and taxation.

Beneficiary Considerations: Consider the needs and circumstances of your beneficiaries, such as their age, financial situation, and potential vulnerabilities. Choose a trust structure that provides the desired level of support and protection for your beneficiaries.

By carefully evaluating the differences between revocable and irrevocable trusts and considering your specific needs and goals, you can make an informed decision that supports your estate planning objectives. Collaborating with experienced legal and financial advisors can help ensure that your trust is structured effectively and provides lasting benefits for you and your beneficiaries.

6.1 Advantages and Disadvantages of Revocable Trusts

Revocable trusts, also known as living trusts, are a popular estate planning tool due to their flexibility and ease of use. They offer several advantages that can simplify the management of your estate during your lifetime and provide clarity in the distribution of assets after death. However, they also come with certain limitations that should be carefully considered. This section outlines the key advantages and disadvantages of revocable trusts to help you determine if they are the right choice for your estate planning needs.

Advantages of Revocable Trusts

Flexibility: One of the most significant advantages of a revocable trust is its flexibility. As the grantor, you retain full control over the trust and its assets during your lifetime. You can amend, modify, or revoke the trust at any time, allowing you to adapt the trust to changing circumstances, such as shifts in financial goals, changes in relationships with beneficiaries, or alterations in the legal environment.

Avoidance of Probate: A revocable trust allows your estate to bypass the probate process, which can be lengthy, costly, and public. Assets held within the trust are distributed according to the trust's terms without the need for court intervention, providing privacy and reducing administrative burdens on your heirs. This can lead to faster distribution of assets to beneficiaries, minimizing delays and costs associated with probate proceedings.

Incapacity Planning: Revocable trusts offer a mechanism for managing your assets if you become incapacitated. By designating a successor trustee in advance, you can ensure that your financial affairs are managed according to your wishes without the need for a court-appointed guardian or conservator. This arrangement can provide peace of mind and protect your interests during periods of incapacity.

Continued Management: After your death, a revocable trust allows for seamless management and distribution of your assets. The trustee can continue to manage the trust's assets according to your instructions, providing stability and continuity for your beneficiaries. This ongoing management can be particularly beneficial if you have minor children, disabled beneficiaries, or complex financial arrangements.

Privacy: Because revocable trusts are not subject to probate, the details of the trust, including its assets and beneficiaries, remain private. This privacy can be advantageous for individuals who wish to keep their financial affairs and distribution plans confidential, as probate proceedings are typically part of the public record.

Disadvantages of Revocable Trusts

No Asset Protection: One of the primary limitations of a revocable trust is that it does not offer protection from creditors. Since you retain control over the trust assets, they are considered part of your estate for liability purposes and can be subject to claims by creditors, lawsuits, and divorce settlements.

No Tax Benefits: Revocable trusts do not provide any tax advantages. The assets within the trust are included in your taxable estate, and any income generated by the trust is reported on your personal income tax return. This means that a revocable trust does not reduce estate or income taxes, although it can be part of a broader tax planning strategy.

Costs and Complexity: Establishing and maintaining a revocable trust involves certain costs and administrative responsibilities. You may incur legal fees for drafting the trust document and additional expenses for ongoing management and compliance. Additionally, all assets must be properly titled in the name of the trust, which can require considerable effort and attention to detail.

Potential for Disputes: While revocable trusts are designed to simplify estate administration, they can still be subject to disputes among beneficiaries. Disagreements may arise over the interpretation of trust terms, the actions of the trustee, or the distribution of assets. Clear communication and well-drafted trust documents can help mitigate these risks, but conflicts may still occur.

Ongoing Management Requirements: Although revocable trusts offer continuity in asset management, they require ongoing oversight to ensure that assets are correctly titled and that the trust reflects your current intentions. This includes regular reviews and updates to the trust document, especially in response to changes in your financial situation, family dynamics, or applicable laws.

Considerations for Choosing a Revocable Trust

When deciding whether a revocable trust is right for you, consider the following factors:

Control and Flexibility: If maintaining control over your assets and having the ability to adapt your estate plan is important to you, a revocable trust may be a suitable choice.

Privacy and Simplicity: If you value privacy and wish to simplify the distribution of your estate, avoiding the probate process through a revocable trust can be beneficial.

Incapacity Planning: For those concerned about managing assets during periods of incapacity, a revocable trust provides a clear mechanism for appointing a trusted individual to handle financial affairs.

Asset Protection Needs: If protecting assets from creditors or legal claims is a primary concern, you may need to explore additional estate planning tools, such as irrevocable trusts, to achieve these goals.

Tax Considerations: While a revocable trust itself does not offer tax benefits, it can be part of a comprehensive estate plan that includes other strategies to minimize taxes. Consulting with a tax advisor can help identify opportunities to optimize your estate plan for tax efficiency.

By carefully weighing the advantages and disadvantages of revocable trusts, you can make an informed decision that aligns with your estate planning goals and personal circumstances. Working with experienced legal and financial advisors can provide valuable insights and ensure that your trust is structured to meet your needs and protect your legacy.

6.2 Advantages and Disadvantages of Irrevocable Trusts

Irrevocable trusts are a powerful estate planning tool that offer significant benefits in terms of asset protection and tax planning. However, they also come with certain limitations due to their inflexible nature. Understanding the advantages and disadvantages of irrevocable trusts can help you decide whether they align with your estate planning goals and personal circumstances.

Advantages of Irrevocable Trusts

Asset Protection: One of the most significant advantages of an irrevocable trust is its ability to protect assets from creditors, lawsuits, and divorce settlements. Once assets are transferred into an irrevocable trust, they are no longer considered part of the grantor's estate, shielding them from claims against the grantor. This protection can be especially valuable for individuals in professions with a high risk of litigation, such as doctors or business owners.

Tax Benefits: Irrevocable trusts can offer substantial tax benefits. By transferring assets out of your estate, you can reduce the size of your taxable estate and potentially lower your estate tax liability. Additionally, income generated by the trust is taxed at the trust's tax rate, which may provide opportunities for tax savings, particularly in cases where the beneficiaries are in lower tax brackets.

Charitable Giving: Irrevocable trusts are an effective vehicle for charitable giving. Establishing a charitable trust, such as a charitable remainder trust or charitable lead trust, allows you to support charitable causes while enjoying tax benefits. You can receive an immediate income tax deduction for the charitable gift and reduce the size of your taxable estate.

Estate Planning Goals: Irrevocable trusts can be tailored to achieve specific estate planning goals, such as preserving wealth for future generations or providing for special needs beneficiaries. For example, a generation-skipping trust can minimize taxes and preserve wealth for grandchildren and future generations. Similarly, a special needs trust can provide for a disabled beneficiary without affecting their eligibility for government benefits.

Reducing Probate Costs and Delays: Like revocable trusts, irrevocable trusts allow assets to bypass probate, which can reduce administrative costs and avoid delays in distributing assets to beneficiaries. This can be particularly beneficial for complex estates or those with assets located in multiple jurisdictions.

Disadvantages of Irrevocable Trusts

Loss of Control: Once assets are transferred into an irrevocable trust, the grantor relinquishes control over them. This means you cannot change the trust's terms or reclaim the assets without the consent of the beneficiaries and the trustee. This lack of flexibility can be a significant disadvantage if your circumstances or goals change.

Complexity and Costs: Establishing and maintaining an irrevocable trust can be complex and costly. The trust document must be carefully drafted to ensure compliance with legal and tax requirements. Additionally, there may be ongoing administrative costs, such as trustee fees and tax filing requirements, which can add to the overall expense.

Irrevocability: The permanent nature of an irrevocable trust can be a drawback if your needs or intentions evolve. Once established, it is challenging to amend or dissolve the trust, which may limit your ability to adapt your estate plan to changing circumstances.

Tax Complications: While irrevocable trusts offer tax benefits, they also come with potential tax complications. The trust must file its own tax returns, and income generated by the trust is subject to trust tax rates, which can be higher than individual rates. Careful planning is needed to manage these tax implications effectively.

Potential for Disputes: Disputes may arise among beneficiaries or between the trustee and beneficiaries regarding the management and distribution of trust assets. Clear communication and well-defined trust terms can help mitigate these risks, but conflicts can still occur.

Considerations for Choosing an Irrevocable Trust

When deciding whether an irrevocable trust is suitable for your estate planning needs, consider the following factors:

Asset Protection Needs: If protecting assets from creditors or legal claims is a priority, an irrevocable trust may be an effective solution. Evaluate the level of protection needed based on your financial situation and risk profile.

Tax Planning Objectives: If reducing estate taxes and optimizing tax efficiency are key goals, an irrevocable trust can be a valuable tool. Work with a tax advisor to assess the potential tax benefits and ensure that the trust is structured to maximize these advantages.

Philanthropic Goals: If you wish to support charitable causes as part of your estate plan, an irrevocable trust can facilitate charitable giving while providing tax benefits. Consider your philanthropic objectives and how a charitable trust can help achieve them.

Control and Flexibility: Consider your comfort level with relinquishing control over assets and the importance of flexibility in your estate plan. If you prefer to maintain control, other estate planning tools, such as revocable trusts or wills, may be more appropriate.

Complexity and Cost Tolerance: Assess your willingness to navigate the complexity and costs associated with establishing and maintaining an irrevocable trust. Ensure that the benefits outweigh the potential drawbacks and align with your overall estate planning strategy.

By carefully evaluating the advantages and disadvantages of irrevocable trusts, you can determine if they are the right fit for your estate planning needs. Consulting with experienced legal and financial advisors can provide valuable insights and ensure that your trust is structured to achieve your goals while providing long-term benefits for you and your beneficiaries.

6.3 Choosing Between Revocable and Irrevocable Trusts

Selecting the right type of trust is a crucial decision in estate planning, as it affects how your assets are managed, protected, and distributed. Revocable and irrevocable trusts each have unique features, benefits, and limitations that cater to different estate planning goals and personal circumstances. This section provides guidance on choosing between these two types of trusts, considering factors such as control, flexibility, asset protection, and tax implications.

Key Considerations for Choosing a Trust

Control and Flexibility

Revocable Trusts: If maintaining control and flexibility over your assets is a priority, a revocable trust may be the better option. It allows you to retain control over the trust assets, make amendments, and revoke the trust entirely if needed. This flexibility is ideal for individuals who anticipate changes in their estate planning needs or who prefer to adjust their plans over time.

Irrevocable Trusts: Irrevocable trusts require you to relinquish control over the trust assets, offering limited flexibility. Once established, the terms of the trust are generally fixed, and changes can only be made with the consent of the beneficiaries and the trustee. This lack of flexibility is suitable for those who have specific, long-term goals and do not foresee significant changes in their estate planning needs.

Asset Protection

Revocable Trusts: Revocable trusts do not offer asset protection, as the assets are considered part of your estate and are subject to claims by creditors, lawsuits, and divorce settlements. If asset protection is a significant concern, a revocable trust may not be the best choice.

Irrevocable Trusts: Irrevocable trusts provide strong asset protection, as the assets are no longer part of your estate and are shielded from creditors and legal claims. This protection is ideal for individuals in professions with high liability risks or those who wish to safeguard their wealth from potential claims.

Tax Planning

Revocable Trusts: Revocable trusts do not offer tax benefits, as the trust assets remain part of your taxable estate. Income generated by the trust is reported on your personal tax return, and the trust does not reduce estate taxes. However, revocable trusts can be part of a comprehensive estate plan that includes other tax-efficient strategies.

Irrevocable Trusts: Irrevocable trusts can offer significant tax benefits by removing assets from your taxable estate and potentially reducing estate and gift taxes. Income generated by the trust is taxed at the trust's rate, which may be advantageous depending on the beneficiaries' tax situations. If tax efficiency is a primary goal, an irrevocable trust may be more appropriate.

Estate Planning Goals

Revocable Trusts: If your primary goals are to avoid probate, manage assets during incapacity, and maintain privacy, a revocable trust may be suitable. It provides continuity in asset management and simplifies the distribution process, making it an effective tool for straightforward estate planning needs.

Irrevocable Trusts: If you have more complex estate planning goals, such as preserving wealth for future generations, providing for special needs beneficiaries, or establishing charitable gifts, an irrevocable trust may be more appropriate. Its ability to achieve specific objectives and offer long-term benefits makes it a powerful tool for complex estate plans.

Beneficiary Considerations

Revocable Trusts: If you anticipate changes in beneficiary designations or wish to retain flexibility in adjusting distributions, a revocable trust may be advantageous. It allows you to easily update beneficiary information and adapt to changes in family dynamics.

Irrevocable Trusts: Irrevocable trusts are well-suited for providing structured support to beneficiaries, such as minors or individuals with special needs. They offer a mechanism for ensuring that assets are managed responsibly and used for the intended purpose, without the risk of beneficiaries accessing funds prematurely.

Steps to Making an Informed Decision

Assess Your Needs and Goals: Begin by assessing your estate planning needs and goals. Consider factors such as your financial situation, family dynamics, risk tolerance, and long-term objectives. Determine whether flexibility, asset protection, or tax efficiency is your primary concern.

Consult with Advisors: Engage with experienced legal, tax, and financial advisors to explore your options and gain insights into the benefits and limitations of each type of trust. Advisors can help you understand the implications of your decision and provide tailored recommendations based on your unique circumstances.

Evaluate Scenarios: Consider different scenarios and how each type of trust would address your specific needs. For example, if you are concerned about potential litigation, evaluate how an irrevocable trust could protect your assets. If you anticipate changes in your family structure, assess how a revocable trust could provide the necessary flexibility.

Consider Hybrid Solutions: In some cases, a combination of revocable and irrevocable trusts may be the best solution. This approach allows you to leverage the benefits of both types of trusts, providing flexibility for certain assets while ensuring protection and tax efficiency for others.

Review and Adjust: Estate planning is an ongoing process that requires regular reviews and adjustments. As your circumstances and goals evolve, continue to evaluate your trust strategy and make updates as needed to ensure it remains aligned with your objectives.

By carefully considering your goals, assessing your needs, and seeking professional guidance, you can choose the trust structure that best aligns with your estate planning strategy. Making an informed decision ensures that your assets are managed and distributed according to your wishes, providing peace of mind for you and your beneficiaries

Chapter 7: Trusts for Special Circumstances

Trusts are versatile tools that can be tailored to meet various estate planning needs, especially in unique or complex situations. Special circumstances often require customized solutions to ensure that assets are managed effectively and that beneficiaries are provided for according to specific needs. This chapter explores different types of trusts designed for special circumstances, highlighting their features, benefits, and considerations.

Special Needs Trusts

A Special Needs Trust (SNT) is designed to provide for beneficiaries with physical or mental disabilities without jeopardizing their eligibility for government benefits such as Medicaid or Supplemental Security Income (SSI). These trusts are crucial for ensuring that disabled beneficiaries receive the necessary support and resources.

Purpose and Benefits: An SNT allows assets to be held in trust for a disabled beneficiary, supplementing government benefits without disqualifying the beneficiary from receiving them. The trust can cover expenses for medical care, education, personal needs, and quality-of-life improvements not covered by public assistance.

Types of Special Needs Trusts:

First-Party Special Needs Trust: Funded with the disabled individual's own assets, such as a personal injury settlement or inheritance. It must comply with federal and state regulations and is subject to a Medicaid payback requirement upon the beneficiary's death.

Third-Party Special Needs Trust: Established and funded by a third party, typically a parent or grandparent, using their own assets. It is not subject to Medicaid payback, allowing the remaining assets to be distributed to other beneficiaries upon the disabled individual's death.

Considerations: When establishing an SNT, it is essential to consult with an attorney experienced in special needs planning to ensure compliance with complex regulations. The trust document must be carefully drafted to meet legal requirements and avoid jeopardizing the beneficiary's eligibility for government benefits.

Charitable Trusts

Charitable trusts are designed to benefit charitable organizations while providing tax benefits to the grantor. They are ideal for individuals who wish to support philanthropic causes as part of their estate plan.

Types of Charitable Trusts:

Charitable Remainder Trust (CRT): Provides income to the grantor or other designated beneficiaries for a specified period, with the remainder of the trust assets going to a designated charity. CRTs offer income tax deductions and can help reduce estate taxes.

Charitable Lead Trust (CLT): Pays income to a charity for a set term, after which the remaining assets are transferred to the grantor's beneficiaries. CLTs can provide gift or estate tax benefits, allowing for the transfer of assets to heirs at a reduced tax cost.

Benefits: Charitable trusts allow the grantor to support charitable causes while enjoying tax advantages. They can help reduce income, estate, and capital gains taxes, depending on the trust structure and assets involved.

Considerations: Establishing a charitable trust requires careful planning to balance philanthropic goals with financial objectives. It is important to work with legal and financial advisors to ensure that the trust is structured to maximize tax benefits and achieve the desired impact.

Spendthrift Trusts

A spendthrift trust is designed to protect a beneficiary's inheritance from creditors and prevent the beneficiary from mismanaging assets. These trusts are often used when the beneficiary lacks financial maturity or has issues with spending or addiction.

Purpose and Benefits: Spendthrift trusts restrict the beneficiary's access to the trust assets, allowing the trustee to control distributions. This protection prevents the beneficiary from squandering the inheritance and shields the assets from creditors.

Trustee's Role: The trustee plays a crucial role in managing the trust assets and determining distributions. It is essential to select a responsible and trustworthy trustee who can balance the beneficiary's needs with the trust's long-term goals.

Considerations: The trust document must include specific spendthrift provisions to limit the beneficiary's control over the trust assets. It is also important to consider potential conflicts between the trustee and beneficiary and ensure clear communication and expectations.

Generation-Skipping Trusts

A Generation-Skipping Trust (GST) is designed to pass wealth directly to grandchildren or subsequent generations, bypassing the grantor's children. This strategy can help minimize estate taxes and preserve family wealth over multiple generations.

Purpose and Benefits: GSTs allow assets to be transferred to grandchildren or later generations without being subject to estate taxes at each generational level. This can result in significant tax savings and preserve family wealth for future generations.

GST Tax Considerations: The Generation-Skipping Transfer Tax (GSTT) applies to transfers to individuals who are two or more generations below the grantor. The GSTT has its own exemption limits, separate from estate and gift tax exemptions, and requires careful planning to maximize benefits.

Trust Structure: GSTs can be structured as dynasty trusts, allowing wealth to be preserved for multiple generations without being subject to estate taxes. This structure requires thoughtful planning and collaboration with legal and financial advisors to ensure compliance with tax laws and to achieve the grantor's long-term goals.

Qualified Personal Residence Trusts

A Qualified Personal Residence Trust (QPRT) is an estate planning tool that allows a grantor to transfer a primary or secondary residence out of their estate while retaining the right to live in the home for a specified period.

Purpose and Benefits: QPRTs can significantly reduce the taxable value of an estate, as the home is transferred at a discounted value based on the retained interest. This strategy can result in substantial estate tax savings while allowing the grantor to continue living in the residence.

Term and Remainder Interest: The grantor retains the right to live in the home for the trust term, after which the property is transferred to designated beneficiaries. The value of the gift is calculated based on the present value of the remainder interest, allowing for potential gift tax savings.

Considerations: A QPRT requires careful planning, as the grantor must survive the trust term for the strategy to be effective. Additionally, the grantor may need to pay rent to the beneficiaries if they wish to continue living in the home after the trust term ends.

Trusts for special circumstances offer tailored solutions for unique estate planning challenges, providing flexibility, protection, and tax advantages. By understanding the various types of trusts available and their specific applications, you can create a comprehensive estate plan that addresses the needs of your beneficiaries and aligns with your long-term goals. Collaborating with experienced legal and financial advisors is essential to ensure that your trust is structured effectively and achieves the desired outcomes.

7.1 Special Needs Trusts: Planning for Beneficiaries with Disabilities

Special Needs Trusts (SNTs) are essential tools in estate planning for families with disabled individuals. These trusts are designed to ensure that beneficiaries with disabilities receive financial support without jeopardizing their eligibility for government benefits such as Medicaid and Supplemental Security Income (SSI). This section explores the types of Special Needs Trusts, their advantages, and the key considerations involved in setting them up.

Types of Special Needs Trusts

There are primarily two types of Special Needs Trusts: First-Party and Third-Party Special Needs Trusts. Each serves different purposes and is funded differently, but both are designed to enhance the quality of life for the beneficiary while preserving access to public benefits.

First-Party Special Needs Trust

Purpose: A First-Party SNT, also known as a self-settled or Medicaid payback trust, is funded with the beneficiary's own assets. This type of trust is typically established when a disabled individual receives a personal injury settlement, inheritance, or has existing assets that could disqualify them from receiving government benefits.

Medicaid Payback Requirement: Upon the death of the beneficiary, any remaining assets in the trust must be used to reimburse the state for Medicaid benefits received by the beneficiary during their lifetime. This payback requirement is a crucial consideration when establishing a First-Party SNT.

Eligibility: To establish a First-Party SNT, the beneficiary must be under the age of 65 at the time the trust is created. The trust must be established by the beneficiary, a parent, grandparent, legal guardian, or a court.

Third-Party Special Needs Trust

Purpose: A Third-Party SNT is funded with assets belonging to someone other than the beneficiary, typically a parent, grandparent, or other family member. This type of trust is often established as part of the family's estate planning to provide long-term financial support for the disabled individual.

No Medicaid Payback Requirement: Unlike First-Party SNTs, Third-Party SNTs are not subject to Medicaid payback provisions. Upon the beneficiary's death, the remaining assets can be distributed to other family members or charities as specified in the trust document.

Flexibility: Third-Party SNTs offer greater flexibility in terms of how assets are managed and distributed. The trust can cover a wide range of expenses that enhance the beneficiary's quality of life, such as education, recreation, personal care, and transportation.

Advantages of Special Needs Trusts

Preservation of Government Benefits: SNTs are specifically designed to ensure that the beneficiary remains eligible for needs-based government benefits such as Medicaid and SSI. By holding assets in the trust, they are not counted as the beneficiary's personal resources, preventing disqualification from these crucial programs.

Enhanced Quality of Life: Special Needs Trusts can provide for a wide range of services and goods that government benefits do not cover, such as specialized therapy, medical equipment, personal care attendants, and recreational activities. This supplemental support significantly enhances the beneficiary's quality of life and independence.

Financial Management and Protection: SNTs offer professional management of trust assets, ensuring that funds are used prudently and in accordance with the beneficiary's needs. The appointed trustee oversees distributions, manages investments, and ensures compliance with legal requirements, protecting the trust assets from potential misuse.

Flexibility in Planning: By establishing an SNT, families can create a flexible estate plan that addresses the unique needs of their disabled loved ones. Trust provisions can be customized to reflect the family's intentions and the beneficiary's specific circumstances.

Key Considerations in Setting Up a Special Needs Trust

Selecting the Right Type of Trust: Determine whether a First-Party or Third-Party SNT is appropriate based on the source of funding and the beneficiary's circumstances. Each type of trust has its own requirements and benefits, and the choice will depend on factors such as asset ownership and Medicaid eligibility.

Choosing a Trustee: The trustee plays a crucial role in managing the trust assets and ensuring that distributions comply with legal requirements. Select a trustee who is knowledgeable about public benefits and understands the beneficiary's needs. This could be a family member, professional fiduciary, or financial institution.

Drafting the Trust Document: The trust document must be carefully drafted to comply with federal and state laws governing SNTs. It should include specific language that outlines the trustee's duties, permissible distributions, and the intended use of trust assets. Consulting with an attorney experienced in special needs planning is essential to ensure compliance and effectiveness.

Regular Reviews and Updates: Periodically review and update the trust document to reflect changes in the beneficiary's needs, family circumstances, or legal landscape. Regular reviews ensure that the trust remains aligned with its intended purpose and continues to provide optimal support for the beneficiary.

Coordinating with Other Benefits: Coordinate the trust with other benefits and resources available to the beneficiary, such as Social Security Disability Insurance (SSDI), private insurance, and community programs. This coordination ensures that the beneficiary receives comprehensive support and maximizes available resources.

By understanding the nuances of Special Needs Trusts and carefully planning their establishment, families can provide financial security and enhance the quality of life for their disabled loved ones. Collaborating with experienced legal and financial professionals ensures that the trust is structured effectively and fulfils its intended purpose, offering peace of mind and long-term protection for the beneficiary.

7.2 Charitable Trusts: Supporting Philanthropy and Reducing Taxes

Charitable trusts are powerful tools for individuals who wish to incorporate philanthropy into their estate planning. These trusts allow you to support charitable causes while enjoying tax benefits, making them an attractive option for those who want to leave a legacy. This section explores the types of charitable trusts, their advantages, and key considerations in establishing them.

Types of Charitable Trusts

There are two main types of charitable trusts: Charitable Remainder Trusts (CRTs) and Charitable Lead Trusts (CLTs). Each type serves different purposes and offers unique benefits, allowing you to tailor your philanthropic goals.

Charitable Remainder Trust (CRT)

Purpose: A CRT allows you to receive income from the trust for a specified period or for your lifetime, with the remainder of the trust assets eventually going to a designated charity or charities. This type of trust is ideal for individuals who want to support charitable causes while maintaining an income stream.

Structure: CRTs can be structured as either an annuity trust (CRAT) or a unitrust (CRUT). In a CRAT, you receive a fixed annual income based on the initial value of the trust. In a CRUT, you receive a variable income based on a fixed percentage of the trust's annually revalued assets.

Tax Benefits: CRTs offer several tax advantages, including an immediate income tax deduction for the present value of the charitable remainder interest. Additionally, appreciated assets transferred to the trust can be sold without incurring capital gains taxes, allowing the full value to be reinvested.

Charitable Lead Trust (CLT)

Purpose: A CLT allows you to transfer assets to a trust that pays income to a designated charity for a specified period, after which the remaining assets are transferred to your heirs or other beneficiaries. This trust is suitable for individuals who want to support charities in the short term while preserving assets for future generations.

Structure: Like CRTs, CLTs can be structured as annuity trusts (CLATs) or unitrusts (CLUTs). In a CLAT, the charity receives a fixed annual payment, while in a CLUT, the charity receives a variable payment based on a fixed percentage of the trust's value.

Tax Benefits: CLTs can provide significant gift and estate tax benefits. The value of the charitable payments reduces the taxable value of the gift, potentially resulting in substantial tax savings. Additionally, any appreciation in the trust's assets during the term is passed on to heirs free of gift or estate tax.

Advantages of Charitable Trusts

Philanthropic Legacy: Charitable trusts enable you to leave a legacy by supporting causes that align with your values and passions. They provide a structured way to make a meaningful impact on charitable organizations and communities.

Tax Benefits: Charitable trusts offer substantial tax advantages, including income tax deductions, avoidance of capital gains taxes on appreciated assets, and potential reductions in estate and gift taxes. These benefits can enhance your overall financial strategy and maximize the value of your charitable contributions.

Income Stream: CRTs provide a reliable income stream for the grantor or other designated beneficiaries, offering financial security while fulfilling philanthropic goals. This feature is particularly beneficial for individuals who need ongoing income during retirement.

Asset Management: Charitable trusts provide professional management of trust assets, ensuring that they are invested wisely and used effectively to achieve your philanthropic objectives. The trustee oversees the trust's operations, distributions, and compliance with legal requirements.

Key Considerations in Establishing a Charitable Trust

Choosing the Right Type of Trust: Determine whether a CRT or CLT aligns better with your goals and financial situation. Consider factors such as the desired income stream, the timing of charitable contributions, and the impact on heirs when selecting the type of trust.

Selecting Charitable Beneficiaries: Identify the charitable organizations you wish to support. Ensure that they align with your values and that their mission reflects your philanthropic intentions. Consider consulting with the charities to understand how your contributions can best support their programs.

Determining the Trust Term: Decide on the duration of the trust. This decision will impact the timing and number of charitable contributions, the income stream for beneficiaries, and the eventual distribution to heirs. The trust term should align with your financial goals and philanthropic vision.

Drafting the Trust Document: Work with an experienced attorney to draft the trust document, ensuring that it complies with legal requirements and accurately reflects your intentions. The document should outline the terms of the trust, the responsibilities of the trustee, and the distribution plan for both charitable and non-charitable beneficiaries.

Appointing a Trustee: Choose a trustee who is knowledgeable about trust administration and tax regulations. The trustee will be responsible for managing the trust assets, making distributions, and ensuring compliance with legal and charitable obligations. Consider appointing a professional trustee or corporate fiduciary to manage complex trusts.

Regular Review and Monitoring: Periodically review the trust's performance and ensure that it continues to align with your philanthropic goals. Regular monitoring helps address changes in financial circumstances, tax laws, and charitable needs. Adjust as needed to optimize the trust's impact and effectiveness.

Charitable trusts are powerful estate planning tools that enable individuals to make a positive impact on society while enjoying significant tax benefits. By understanding the differences between CRTs and CLTs, you can select the trust structure that best aligns with your philanthropic vision and financial goals. Collaborating with experienced legal and financial advisors ensures that your charitable trust is effectively established and managed, providing lasting benefits for both your beneficiaries and the charitable causes you support.

7.3 Spendthrift Trusts: Protecting Beneficiaries from Themselves

Spendthrift trusts are an important estate planning tool for individuals who wish to provide for beneficiaries who may lack the financial maturity or responsibility to manage their inheritances wisely. These trusts offer protection against impulsive spending, creditors, and legal claims, ensuring that the assets are preserved and used according to the grantor's intentions. This section explores the features, advantages, and considerations of spendthrift trusts.

Purpose and Features of Spendthrift Trusts

A spendthrift trust is designed to safeguard a beneficiary's inheritance by placing restrictions on how and when the trust assets can be accessed. The trust includes specific provisions that limit the beneficiary's control over the assets, protecting them from potential financial mismanagement and external threats.

Limited Access to Assets: The key feature of a spendthrift trust is its ability to restrict the beneficiary's access to trust assets. The trust document specifies how much and when distributions can be made, preventing the beneficiary from accessing large sums of money at once.

Protection from Creditors: Spendthrift provisions protect the trust assets from the beneficiary's creditors. Since the beneficiary does not have direct control over the assets, creditors cannot claim them to satisfy debts or judgments. This protection is especially important for beneficiaries who may be vulnerable to legal claims or financial exploitation.

Trustee Control: The trustee manages the trust assets and makes distributions to the beneficiary according to the trust's terms. The trustee's role is crucial in ensuring that the trust funds are used appropriately and in the best interest of the beneficiary.

Preservation of Wealth: By limiting access to the trust assets, a spendthrift trust helps preserve wealth for the beneficiary's long-term needs. The trust can provide financial support for specific purposes, such as education, healthcare, or living expenses, without the risk of depletion due to poor financial decisions.

Advantages of Spendthrift Trusts

Financial Discipline: Spendthrift trusts encourage financial discipline by controlling the timing and number of distributions. Beneficiaries receive funds in a structured manner, reducing the temptation for impulsive spending and fostering responsible financial behaviour.

Asset Protection: The trust provides robust asset protection, shielding the trust assets from the beneficiary's creditors and legal claims. This protection ensures that the funds are used for their intended purposes and remain available for the beneficiary's long-term support.

Tailored Support: The trust can be customized to meet the beneficiary's specific needs and circumstances. Grantors can include provisions for special situations, such as medical emergencies or educational expenses, ensuring that the trust provides meaningful support.

Peace of Mind: For grantors, a spendthrift trust offers peace of mind knowing that their beneficiaries are financially secure and protected from potential threats. The trust ensures that the assets are managed responsibly and according to the grantor's wishes.

Key Considerations in Establishing a Spendthrift Trust

Drafting the Trust Document: The trust document must be carefully drafted to include clear spendthrift provisions and outline the trustee's duties and powers. It should specify the conditions for distributions and any restrictions on the beneficiary's access to trust assets.

Selecting a Trustee: Choosing the right trustee is critical for the effective management of a spendthrift trust. The trustee should be responsible, trustworthy, and capable of making informed decisions in the beneficiary's best interest. Consider appointing a professional trustee or corporate fiduciary if family dynamics or potential conflicts are a concern.

Balancing Control and Flexibility: While the primary purpose of a spendthrift trust is to restrict access to assets, it is important to strike a balance between control and flexibility. The trust should allow for discretionary distributions in exceptional circumstances, ensuring that the beneficiary's needs are met without compromising the trust's protective features.

Understanding Legal Limitations: Spendthrift trusts must comply with state laws, which can vary in their recognition and enforcement of spendthrift provisions. Consult with an attorney experienced in trust law to ensure that the trust is structured in compliance with applicable legal requirements.

Regular Reviews and Updates: Periodically review the trust document to ensure it continues to meet the beneficiary's needs and aligns with the grantor's intentions. Life changes, such as the beneficiary gaining financial maturity or changes in family circumstances, may necessitate updates to the trust terms.

Communicating with the Beneficiary: While the beneficiary may not have direct control over the trust assets, open communication about the trust's purpose and terms can help manage expectations and foster a positive relationship between the beneficiary and the trustee. Clear communication can also prevent misunderstandings and conflicts.

Spendthrift trusts are effective tools for protecting beneficiaries from financial mismanagement and external threats. By limiting access to trust assets and providing structured support, these trusts ensure that beneficiaries receive the financial assistance they need while safeguarding their inheritance for the future. Collaborating with experienced legal and financial professionals is essential to establish a spendthrift trust that meets the grantor's objectives and provides lasting benefits for the beneficiary.

Chapter 8: The Role of the Trustee in Trust Administration

The trustee plays a crucial role in the administration of a trust, serving as the legal representative responsible for managing the trust's assets and ensuring that the terms of the trust are carried out according to the grantor's wishes. This chapter explores the responsibilities, qualities, and challenges of being a trustee, as well as the steps involved in effective trust administration.

Responsibilities of the Trustee

A trustee has several key responsibilities that are essential to the proper functioning of the trust. These duties require a high level of integrity, diligence, and transparency.

Fiduciary Duty: The trustee has a fiduciary duty to act in the best interests of the beneficiaries. This duty requires the trustee to manage the trust assets with care, loyalty, and impartiality. The trustee must prioritize the beneficiaries' needs and adhere to the terms of the trust document.

Asset Management: The trustee is responsible for managing the trust's assets, which includes investing funds, collecting income, and preserving the trust's value. The trustee must make prudent investment decisions that align with the trust's objectives and the beneficiaries' needs.

Record-Keeping and Reporting: Accurate record-keeping is essential for effective trust administration. The trustee must maintain detailed records of all transactions, distributions, and financial statements. Regular reporting to beneficiaries ensures transparency and helps build trust.

Distributions: The trustee is responsible for making distributions to beneficiaries according to the terms of the trust. This includes determining the appropriate timing and number of distributions and ensuring that they align with the trust's objectives.

Tax Compliance: The trustee must ensure that the trust complies with all applicable tax laws. This involves preparing and filing tax returns for the trust and paying any taxes owed. Proper tax management is crucial to preserving the trust's assets and minimizing liabilities.

Communication with Beneficiaries: The trustee must maintain open communication with beneficiaries, providing them with information about the trust's status and responding to their inquiries. Effective communication helps manage expectations and prevent conflicts.

Qualities of an Effective Trustee

An effective trustee possesses several qualities that enable them to fulfil their responsibilities and manage the trust successfully:

Integrity: Trustworthiness and honesty are paramount for a trustee. The trustee must always adhere to ethical standards and act in the beneficiaries' best interests.

Financial Acumen: A good trustee has a solid understanding of financial management and investment principles. This knowledge is essential for making informed decisions about asset management and ensuring the trust's financial health.

Impartiality: The trustee must act impartially, treating all beneficiaries fairly and without favouritism. This requires balancing the needs and interests of multiple beneficiaries and making objective decisions.

Attention to Detail: Effective trustees pay close attention to detail, ensuring that all aspects of trust administration are handled accurately and efficiently.

This includes meticulous record-keeping and adherence to legal and tax requirements.

Communication Skills: Strong communication skills are essential for interacting with beneficiaries, advisors, and other stakeholders. The trustee must be able to convey information clearly and address any concerns or questions.

Challenges Faced by Trustees

Trustees may encounter various challenges during the administration of a trust. Anticipating and addressing these challenges is crucial for successful trust management.

Conflicting Interests: Balancing the interests of multiple beneficiaries can be challenging, especially when their needs or expectations differ. The trustee must navigate these conflicts and make decisions that align with the trust's objectives.

Complex Legal and Tax Issues: Trusts often involve complex legal and tax considerations that require specialized knowledge. Trustees may need to work with legal and financial advisors to ensure compliance and optimize the trust's management.

Managing Risk: Trustees must manage investment risk while striving to achieve the trust's financial goals. This involves developing a diversified investment strategy and regularly reviewing the trust's performance.

Beneficiary Disputes: Disputes among beneficiaries can arise over distributions, trust terms, or other issues. The trustee must address these disputes promptly and fairly, often requiring mediation or legal intervention.

Administrative Burden: The administrative responsibilities of a trustee can be time-consuming and complex. Trustees must be diligent in fulfilling their duties and staying organized to avoid errors and ensure efficient administration.

Steps for Effective Trust Administration

To effectively administer a trust, trustees should follow a structured approach that includes the following steps:

Review the Trust Document: Begin by thoroughly reviewing the trust document to understand its terms, objectives, and the trustee's responsibilities. This foundational knowledge is crucial for effective administration.

Inventory Assets: Create a comprehensive inventory of the trust's assets, including real estate, financial accounts, investments, and personal property. Ensure that all assets are properly titled in the name of the trust.

Develop an Investment Strategy: Work with financial advisors to develop an investment strategy that aligns with the trust's goals and the beneficiaries' needs. Regularly review and adjust the strategy to respond to changing market conditions and circumstances.

Establish Record-Keeping Practices: Implement a system for maintaining detailed records of all transactions, communications, and financial reports. This ensures transparency and facilitates efficient administration.

Communicate with Beneficiaries: Establish open lines of communication with beneficiaries, providing regular updates on the trust's status and responding to their inquiries. Transparency builds trust and helps manage expectations.

Ensure Legal and Tax Compliance: Stay informed about legal and tax obligations related to the trust. Work with legal and tax advisors to ensure compliance and optimize the trust's management for tax efficiency.

Plan for Contingencies: Anticipate potential challenges and develop contingency plans to address them. This may include appointing successor trustees or establishing protocols for managing disputes.

Conduct Regular Reviews: Periodically review the trust's performance and administration to ensure that it remains aligned with its objectives and the beneficiaries' needs. Adjust as needed to optimize management.

The ole of the trustee is integral to the success of a trust. By fulfilling their fiduciary responsibilities with diligence and integrity, trustees ensure that the trust operates smoothly and achieves its intended goals. Collaborating with legal, financial, and tax advisors can provide valuable support and guidance, helping trustees navigate the complexities of trust administration and provide for the beneficiaries according to the grantor's wishes.

8.1 Selecting the Right Trustee: Considerations and Best Practices

Choosing the right trustee is one of the most critical decisions in establishing a trust. The trustee is responsible for managing the trust's assets, ensuring compliance with legal requirements, and fulfilling the grantor's intentions. Selecting an appropriate trustee requires careful consideration of the trustee's qualities, the needs of the beneficiaries, and the complexity of the trust. This section explores key considerations and best practices for selecting the right trustee.

Qualities to Look for in a Trustee

When selecting a trustee, it is important to evaluate candidates based on the following key qualities:

Integrity and Trustworthiness

Ethical Standards: The trustee must possess a strong sense of integrity and adhere to high ethical standards. They are entrusted with significant responsibilities and must always act in the best interests of the beneficiaries.

Reputation: Consider the reputation and track record of potential trustees. Trustworthiness and reliability are crucial traits that ensure the trustee can be relied upon to manage the trust assets responsibly.

Financial Acumen

Investment Knowledge: A good trustee should have a solid understanding of financial management and investment principles. This knowledge is essential for making informed decisions about managing the trust's assets and ensuring their growth and preservation.

Analytical Skills: The trustee should possess strong analytical skills to evaluate investment opportunities, assess risks, and optimize the trust's financial performance.

Impartiality and Fairness

Objectivity: The trustee must act impartially, treating all beneficiaries fairly and without favoritism. They should be able to make objective decisions that balance the needs and interests of multiple beneficiaries.

Conflict Resolution: The ability to manage and resolve conflicts among beneficiaries is essential. The trustee should be skilled in addressing disputes and ensuring that the trust's terms are carried out equitably.

Attention to Detail

Precision: Effective trustees pay close attention to detail, ensuring that all aspects of trust administration are handled accurately and efficiently. This includes meticulous record-keeping and adherence to legal and tax requirements.

Organizational Skills: Strong organizational skills are necessary to manage the trust's assets, documents, and reporting efficiently.

Communication Skills

Transparency: The trustee must maintain open and transparent communication with beneficiaries, providing them with information about the trust's status and responding to their inquiries.

Interpersonal Skills: Strong interpersonal skills help foster positive relationships with beneficiaries and facilitate effective collaboration with advisors and other stakeholders.

Types of Trustees

When selecting a trustee, consider the following options based on the complexity of the trust and the specific needs of the beneficiaries:

Individual Trustee

Family Member or Friend: Choosing a trusted family member or friend as a trustee can provide personal insight into the beneficiaries' needs and family dynamics. However, consider whether they have the necessary skills and knowledge to manage the trust effectively.

Advantages: Individual trustees often have a personal connection to the beneficiaries and may be more attuned to their needs and preferences.

Challenges: Individual trustees may lack the expertise required for complex financial management, and personal biases or conflicts of interest could arise.

Professional Trustee

Financial Advisor or Lawyer: A professional trustee, such as a financial advisor or attorney, offers expertise in managing trust assets and navigating legal and tax obligations.

Advantages: Professional trustees bring a high level of expertise and objectivity to trust management. They can handle complex financial situations and ensure compliance with legal requirements.

Challenges: Professional trustees may charge fees for their services, which can increase the administrative costs of the trust.

Corporate Trustee

Trust Companies and Banks: Corporate trustees are institutions that specialize in trust administration. They offer comprehensive services, including asset management, tax compliance, and beneficiary communication.

Advantages: Corporate trustees provide a high level of expertise, continuity, and objectivity. They have the resources and experience to manage complex trusts effectively.

Challenges: Corporate trustees may have less personal connection with beneficiaries and can be more expensive than individual or professional trustees.

Best Practices for Selecting a Trustee

Assess the Complexity of the Trust: Consider the complexity of the trust's assets and the specific needs of the beneficiaries when selecting a trustee. Complex trusts may require the expertise of a professional or corporate trustee, while simpler trusts may be effectively managed by a trusted individual.

Evaluate Potential Conflicts of Interest: Assess potential trustees for any conflicts of interest that could impact their ability to act impartially. Choose a trustee who can manage the trust assets objectively and without bias.

Consider the Long-Term Needs of Beneficiaries: Ensure that the trustee can manage the trust for the long term, taking into account the evolving needs and circumstances of the beneficiaries. Consider appointing a successor trustee to ensure continuity in trust management.

Review the Trustee's Experience and Qualifications: Evaluate the experience and qualifications of potential trustees, particularly in areas such as financial management, investment strategies, and legal compliance. Choose a trustee with the skills and expertise necessary to manage the trust effectively.

Conduct Interviews and Gather References: Interview potential trustees and gather references to assess their suitability for the role. Ask questions about their experience, approach to trust management, and ability to handle complex situations.

Establish Clear Expectations: Clearly communicate the responsibilities and expectations for the trustee. Ensure that the trustee understands the terms of the trust document and is committed to fulfilling their duties in accordance with the grantor's intentions.

Selecting the right trustee is a crucial step in ensuring the successful administration of a trust. By carefully considering the qualities, experience, and capabilities of potential trustees, you can make an informed decision that aligns with the trust's objectives and the beneficiaries' needs. Collaborating with experienced legal and financial advisors can provide valuable guidance in the selection process, ensuring that the chosen trustee is well-equipped to manage the trust and fulfil the grantor's intentions.

8.2 Trustee Responsibilities: Duties and Best Practices

Once a trustee is appointed, they have a legal obligation to manage the trust assets in accordance with the trust document and in the best interests of the beneficiaries. This section outlines the core responsibilities of a trustee and offers best practices to ensure effective and compliant trust administration.

Core Responsibilities of a Trustee

Fiduciary Duty

Loyalty to Beneficiaries: The trustee must prioritize the interests of the beneficiaries over their own. This requires making decisions that benefit the beneficiaries and avoiding conflicts of interest.

Prudent Management: The trustee must manage the trust assets prudently, like how a reasonably careful person would manage their own financial affairs. This involves careful investment decisions and risk management.

Asset Management

Investment Strategy: Develop and implement an investment strategy that aligns with the trust's goals and the needs of the beneficiaries. Regularly review and adjust the strategy in response to market conditions and changes in the beneficiaries' circumstances.

Diversification: Ensure that the trust's investment portfolio is diversified to minimize risk and optimize returns. Diversification helps protect the trust's assets from market volatility.

Record-Keeping and Reporting

Accurate Documentation: Maintain detailed records of all trust transactions, including receipts, disbursements, and investments. This documentation is crucial for transparency and accountability.

Regular Reports: Provide regular financial reports to beneficiaries, detailing the trust's performance, distributions, and any significant changes. Clear reporting helps build trust and keeps beneficiaries informed.

Distributions

Adhering to Trust Terms: Make distributions to beneficiaries according to the terms specified in the trust document. This includes determining the timing and number of distributions based on the trust's objectives and the beneficiaries' needs.

Discretionary Distributions: If the trust grants the trustee discretionary authority over distributions, exercise this discretion wisely and impartially, considering the beneficiaries' circumstances and the overall goals of the trust.

Tax Compliance

Filing Tax Returns: Prepare and file the necessary tax returns for the trust. This includes federal and state income tax returns and, if applicable, estate tax filings. Proper tax compliance helps avoid penalties and minimizes the trust's tax liabilities.

Tax Planning: Work with tax advisors to optimize the trust's tax position. This may involve strategies to minimize income and estate taxes, taking advantage of available deductions and credits.

Communication with Beneficiaries

Open Dialogue: Maintain open lines of communication with beneficiaries, addressing their questions and concerns promptly. Transparency fosters trust and reduces the likelihood of disputes.

Managing Expectations: Set clear expectations for beneficiaries regarding the trust's objectives, distribution policies, and any limitations or restrictions.

Best Practices for Effective Trust Administration

Understand the Trust Document: Begin by thoroughly reviewing the trust document to understand its terms, objectives, and the trustee's responsibilities. This foundational knowledge is essential for effective administration.

Stay Informed: Keep up to date with changes in laws and regulations that may affect trust administration. This includes tax laws, fiduciary standards, and any relevant legal developments. Regular consultations with legal and financial advisors can provide valuable insights.

Develop a Management Plan: Create a comprehensive management plan that outlines the investment strategy, distribution schedule, and administrative processes. This plan serves as a roadmap for trust administration and ensures consistency in decision-making.

Use Professional Advisors: Collaborate with experienced legal, financial, and tax advisors to support trust administration. Advisors can provide expertise in areas such as investment management, tax planning, and legal compliance.

Monitor Trust Performance: Regularly review the trust's financial performance and adjust as needed to align with the trust's objectives and the beneficiaries' needs. This includes assessing investment returns, distribution policies, and overall financial health.

Prepare for Contingencies: Anticipate potential challenges and develop contingency plans to address them. This may include appointing successor trustees, establishing protocols for handling disputes, and ensuring that the trust remains resilient in the face of unforeseen events.

Foster Beneficiary Relationships: Build positive relationships with beneficiaries by maintaining open communication, providing clear information, and addressing any concerns promptly. A strong relationship with beneficiaries helps prevent misunderstandings and fosters a collaborative approach to trust administration.

Maintain Confidentiality: Protect the privacy of the trust and its beneficiaries by maintaining confidentiality regarding trust matters. This includes safeguarding sensitive financial information and respecting the privacy of beneficiary communications.

The responsibilities of a trustee are complex and require a high level of diligence, integrity, and expertise. By understanding and fulfilling these responsibilities, trustees can effectively manage the trust assets and ensure that the trust operates in accordance with the grantor's intentions. Collaborating with professional advisors and adhering to best practices can enhance trust administration, providing beneficiaries with financial security and peace of mind

8.3 Challenges and Solutions in Trust Administration

Administering a trust can be a complex and demanding task that involves navigating legal, financial, and interpersonal challenges. Trustees must be prepared to address these challenges effectively to fulfil their fiduciary duties and ensure that the trust operates smoothly. This section explores common challenges faced by trustees and offers practical solutions for overcoming them.

Common Challenges in Trust Administration

Conflicting Interests Among Beneficiaries

Nature of the Challenge: Trustees often face situations where beneficiaries have differing needs, priorities, or expectations. These conflicts can arise over distribution amounts, timing, or perceived fairness in the management of trust assets.

Solution: Establish clear communication channels with beneficiaries to understand their concerns and expectations. Hold regular meetings to discuss the trust's objectives and distribution policies. Encourage open dialogue to foster understanding and collaboration. When necessary, seek mediation or professional advice to resolve conflicts impartially.

Complex Investment Decisions

Nature of the Challenge: Trustees are responsible for managing the trust's investments to achieve growth and preserve capital. Market volatility, economic uncertainties, and changing beneficiary needs can complicate investment decisions.

Solution: Develop a well-defined investment strategy that aligns with the trust's objectives and risk tolerance. Collaborate with financial advisors to create a diversified portfolio that balances growth and risk. Regularly review the investment performance and adjust the strategy as needed to respond to market conditions and beneficiaries' changing circumstances.

Legal and Regulatory Compliance

Nature of the Challenge: Trusts are subject to complex legal and regulatory requirements, including tax laws, fiduciary standards, and reporting obligations. Non-compliance can result in penalties, legal disputes, and damage to the trust's reputation.

Solution: Stay informed about changes in laws and regulations affecting trust administration. Work with legal and tax advisors to ensure compliance and address any legal issues promptly. Implement robust record-keeping and reporting practices to maintain transparency and accountability.

Managing Distributions

Nature of the Challenge: Trustees must balance the need to provide financial support to beneficiaries with the responsibility to preserve the trust's assets for future needs. Discretionary distribution decisions can be particularly challenging when beneficiaries have differing financial situations or expectations.

Solution: Adhere to the distribution guidelines outlined in the trust document. Consider the long-term financial stability of the trust when making distribution decisions. Communicate openly with beneficiaries about the rationale for distribution amounts and timing. If the trust grants discretionary authority, use it judiciously, considering the beneficiaries' unique circumstances and needs.

Potential for Beneficiary Disputes

Nature of the Challenge: Disputes among beneficiaries can arise over perceived inequities, misunderstandings about the trust's terms, or dissatisfaction with the trustee's decisions. These disputes can disrupt trust administration and lead to legal challenges.

Solution: Foster a transparent and inclusive decision-making process by regularly communicating with beneficiaries and providing clear explanations for trustee actions. Encourage beneficiaries to express their concerns and address them promptly and fairly. If disputes escalate, consider engaging a neutral third-party mediator to facilitate resolution.

Trustee Liability and Risk Management

Nature of the Challenge: Trustees are exposed to potential liability for breaches of fiduciary duty, errors in administration, or investment losses. Managing these risks is crucial to protect the trustee's personal assets and the trust's integrity.

Solution: Implement risk management practices, such as obtaining liability insurance to cover potential claims. Adhere to fiduciary standards and document all decisions and actions related to trust administration. Regularly review the trust's financial statements and performance to identify and address any potential issues.

Time and Resource Constraints

Nature of the Challenge: Trust administration can be time-consuming, requiring significant attention to detail and coordination with various stakeholders. Trustees may face challenges balancing their responsibilities with other personal or professional commitments.

Solution: Establish efficient administrative processes and delegate tasks where appropriate. Consider hiring professional advisors, such as accountants, financial planners, or trust officers, to assist with complex aspects of trust administration. Set realistic timelines and prioritize tasks to ensure effective management of the trust's responsibilities.

Strategies for Successful Trust Administration

Education and Training: Invest in ongoing education and training to enhance your knowledge of trust administration, legal requirements, and investment strategies. Attend seminars, workshops, and courses to stay updated on best practices and emerging trends.

Regular Reviews and Audits: Conduct regular reviews and audits of the trust's financial performance, legal compliance, and administrative processes. This proactive approach helps identify areas for improvement and ensures that the trust remains aligned with its objectives.

Technology Utilization: Leverage technology to streamline trust administration, improve communication, and enhance record-keeping. Use financial management software, secure document-sharing platforms, and digital communication tools to facilitate efficient administration.

Building a Strong Advisory Team: Assemble a team of experienced legal, financial, and tax advisors to provide guidance and support in managing the trust. A strong advisory team can help navigate complex issues, optimize trust performance, and ensure compliance with legal and regulatory requirements.

Establishing Clear Policies and Procedures: Develop clear policies and procedures for trust administration, including guidelines for decision-making, risk management, and beneficiary communication. Documenting these processes helps ensure consistency and transparency in trust management.

By understanding and addressing the challenges of trust administration, trustees can effectively fulfil their responsibilities and ensure the successful operation of the trust. Implementing best practices and leveraging the expertise of professional advisors can enhance trust administration, providing beneficiaries with financial security and peace of mind.

Chapter 9: Estate Planning Beyond Trusts

While trusts are powerful tools for managing and distributing assets, comprehensive estate planning encompasses a broader range of strategies and instruments. Effective estate planning involves a holistic approach that includes wills, powers of attorney, healthcare directives, and considerations for tax efficiency. This chapter explores these additional elements of estate planning to ensure that your assets are protected, and your wishes are honoured.

The Importance of a Will

A will is a foundational document in estate planning that outlines how your assets will be distributed upon your death. Even if you have a trust, a will serves several essential functions:

Pour-Over Will: For those with a revocable trust, a pour-over will can be used to transfer any remaining assets into the trust upon death. This ensures that all assets are managed and distributed according to the trust's terms.

Guardianship for Minors: A will allows you to designate guardians for minor children. This provision is crucial for ensuring that your children are cared for by trusted individuals in the event of your untimely passing.

Distribution of Personal Property: A will can specify the distribution of personal belongings and sentimental items that may not be covered by a trust. This clarity helps prevent disputes among heirs.

Executor Appointment: A will allows you to appoint an executor to oversee the administration of your estate. The executor ensures that your wishes are carried out, debts are settled, and assets are distributed as specified.

Powers of Attorney

Powers of attorney (POA) are legal documents that designate someone to make decisions on your behalf if you become incapacitated. They are crucial for ensuring continuity in managing your affairs when you are unable to do so.

Financial Power of Attorney: This document grants an agent the authority to manage your financial affairs, including paying bills, managing investments, and handling real estate transactions. It is essential for ensuring that your financial obligations are met and that your assets are protected.

Durable Power of Attorney: A durable power of attorney remains in effect even if you become incapacitated. This durability ensures that your agent can continue to manage your affairs without interruption, providing peace of mind and stability.

Choosing an Agent: Select an agent who is trustworthy, financially savvy, and capable of making sound decisions in your best interest. It is also wise to appoint a successor agent in case your primary choice is unable or unwilling to serve.

Healthcare Directives

Healthcare directives, also known as advance directives, provide instructions for your medical care if you are unable to communicate your wishes. These documents are vital for ensuring that your healthcare preferences are respected.

Living Will: A living will outline your preferences for medical treatment in situations where you are unable to make decisions, such as terminal illness or permanent unconsciousness. It can specify treatments you do or do not want, such as resuscitation or life support.

Healthcare Power of Attorney: This document appoints an agent to make healthcare decisions on your behalf if you are incapacitated. The agent is responsible for ensuring that your medical care aligns with your values and wishes.

Communicating Your Wishes: It is crucial to discuss your healthcare preferences with your designated agent and family members. Open communication ensures that everyone understands your wishes and reduces the likelihood of conflicts or misunderstandings.

Considerations for Tax Efficiency

Estate planning is not just about asset distribution; it also involves strategies to minimize taxes and preserve wealth for your heirs. Here are some key considerations for achieving tax efficiency:

Gift Tax Exemptions: Take advantage of annual gift tax exemptions to transfer wealth to heirs during your lifetime. This strategy reduces the size of your taxable estate and provides financial support to beneficiaries.

Lifetime Exclusion Amount: The federal estate tax allows for a significant lifetime exclusion amount, which can be used to transfer assets tax-free. Properly planning for the use of this exclusion can minimize estate taxes and maximize the inheritance for your heirs.

Charitable Contributions: Making charitable contributions can reduce your taxable estate and provide income tax deductions. Charitable trusts and donor-advised funds are effective tools for incorporating philanthropy into your estate plan.

Qualified Personal Residence Trust (QPRT): A QPRT allows you to transfer your home to heirs at a reduced gift tax value while retaining the right to live in the property for a specified period. This strategy can significantly reduce estate taxes on an asset.

Tax-Deferred Accounts: Consider the impact of tax-deferred accounts, such as IRAs and 401(k)s, on your estate plan. Designate beneficiaries for these accounts to ensure they are transferred efficiently and consider Roth conversions to manage future tax liabilities.

Business Succession Planning

For business owners, estate planning must include strategies for business succession to ensure the continuity of the enterprise and the protection of its value.

Succession Plan: Develop a formal succession plan that outlines the transition of ownership and management responsibilities. This plan should identify successors, specify training and development needs, and establish a timeline for the transition.

Buy-Sell Agreements: A buy-sell agreement is a contract that outlines the terms for the sale or transfer of business ownership upon specific triggering events, such as retirement, disability, or death. It provides a clear framework for managing ownership changes and protects the business from disruption.

Valuation of Business Interests: Regularly assess the value of your business interests to ensure accurate estate planning and fair distribution to heirs. Professional valuations provide a reliable basis for decision-making and negotiations.

Involving Family Members: Engage family members in discussions about the future of the business and their roles in it. Open communication and collaboration foster alignment and ensure that family dynamics are considered in the planning process.

Estate planning beyond trusts involves a comprehensive approach that addresses various aspects of your financial and personal affairs. By incorporating wills, powers of attorney, healthcare directives, tax-efficient strategies, and business succession planning, you can create a robust estate plan that protects your assets, honours your wishes, and provides for your loved ones. Collaborating with experienced legal and financial advisors ensures that your estate plan is tailored to your unique circumstances and achieves your long-term goals

9.1 The Role of Wills in Comprehensive Estate Planning

Wills are fundamental components of estate planning that ensure your wishes are honoured regarding the distribution of your assets and the guardianship of your minor children. While trusts offer various advantages in managing assets and avoiding probate, wills remain essential for addressing specific aspects of your estate that trusts cannot. This section explores the critical role of wills in estate planning, including their functions, advantages, and integration with other estate planning tools.

Functions of a Will

Asset Distribution

Directing Inheritance: A will specifies how your assets are to be distributed upon your death. This includes real estate, personal property, financial accounts, and any other possessions you wish to pass on to beneficiaries.

Beneficiary Designations: You can name specific individuals or entities, such as charities, to receive assets, ensuring that your distribution wishes are clear and legally enforceable.

Appointment of Guardians

Guardianship for Minors: A will allows you to designate guardians for your minor children. This designation ensures that your children are cared for by individuals you trust if you are no longer able to do so.

Contingency Planning: You can also appoint alternate guardians in case your primary choice is unable or unwilling to serve, providing an additional layer of security for your children's future.

Executor Appointment

Choosing an Executor: A will allows you to appoint an executor, the person responsible for managing your estate, settling debts, and distributing assets according to your instructions. Selecting a reliable and competent executor is crucial for ensuring that your estate is handled efficiently and in accordance with your wishes.

Alternate Executors: You can name alternate executors to serve in case your primary choice is unable or unwilling to fulfil the role, ensuring continuity in estate administration.

Handling Debts and Taxes

Settling Liabilities: A will provides instructions for settling outstanding debts and taxes from your estate. The executor is responsible for using estate assets to pay these obligations before distributing the remaining assets to beneficiaries.

Specific Instructions: You can include specific instructions on how to handle certain debts or tax obligations, providing clarity and guidance for the executor.

Advantages of Having a Will

Clarity and Certainty

Reducing Ambiguity: A well-drafted will reduces ambiguity and provides clear instructions for the distribution of your assets, minimizing potential disputes among heirs.

Legal Enforceability: A will is a legally binding document that ensures your wishes are respected and carried out as intended.

Flexibility

Updating and Amending: Wills can be updated and amended throughout your lifetime, allowing you to adjust your estate plan in response to changing circumstances, such as marriage, divorce, or the birth of a child.

Comprehensive Planning: Wills can address a wide range of issues beyond asset distribution, including guardianship, charitable donations, and specific bequests.

Integration with Trusts

Pour-Over Wills: For individuals with revocable trusts, a pour-over will ensures that any assets not already transferred to the trust during your lifetime are transferred upon your death. This integration helps streamline estate administration and ensures that all assets are managed according to the trust's terms.

Complementary Roles: Wills and trusts can work together to provide comprehensive estate planning solutions. While trusts offer advantages such as probate avoidance and asset protection, wills address aspects that trusts cannot, such as guardianship and personal property distribution.

Drafting a Will

Consulting an Attorney

Legal Expertise: Engaging an experienced estate planning attorney is essential for drafting a will that meets legal requirements and accurately reflects your intentions. An attorney can help you navigate complex legal issues and ensure that your will is enforceable.

Customizing the Document: An attorney can tailor the will to your specific needs, incorporating provisions that address your unique circumstances and goals.

Identifying Assets and Beneficiaries

Comprehensive Inventory: Create a comprehensive inventory of your assets, including real estate, personal property, financial accounts, and any other possessions you wish to include in your will.

Designating Beneficiaries: Clearly specify the individuals or entities you wish to inherit your assets, ensuring that your distribution wishes are clear and unambiguous.

Reviewing and Updating the Will

Regular Reviews: Regularly review your will to ensure it remains current and reflects any changes in your circumstances, such as marriage, divorce, the birth of a child, or significant financial changes.

Amendments: Amend the will as necessary to update beneficiary designations, executor appointments, or any other provisions that require adjustment.

Executing the Will

Legal Formalities: Ensure that the will is executed according to the legal requirements of your state, including signing the document in the presence of witnesses and, if required, having it notarized.

Safekeeping: Store the original will in a safe and accessible location, such as a fireproof safe or with your attorney. Inform your executor and trusted family members of its location.

Limitations of a Will

Probate Process
Probate Requirement: Unlike trusts, wills are subject to the probate process, which can be time-consuming, costly, and public. Probate involves court supervision of the distribution of assets, and its complexity varies by state.

Strategies for Avoidance: Consider complementing your will with other estate planning tools, such as trusts or joint ownership arrangements, to minimize the impact of probate.

Limited Asset Protection

Creditor Claims: Assets distributed through a will are subject to creditor claims, meaning that debts and liabilities must be settled before beneficiaries receive their inheritances.

Incorporating Trusts: To enhance asset protection, consider using trusts to hold and manage assets, providing an additional layer of security against creditor claims.

Wills are indispensable elements of comprehensive estate planning, providing clarity and legal certainty for the distribution of assets and the care of minor children. By integrating wills with other estate planning tools, such as trusts and powers of attorney, individuals can create a robust and flexible estate plan that addresses all aspects of their financial and personal affairs. Collaborating with experienced legal professionals ensures that wills are drafted accurately and effectively, protecting your legacy and providing for your loved ones.

9.2 Powers of Attorney and Healthcare Directives: Ensuring Your Wishes Are Honoured

In addition to wills and trusts, powers of attorney and healthcare directives are essential components of comprehensive estate planning. These legal documents ensure that your financial and medical decisions are handled according to your wishes if you become incapacitated. This section explores the role and importance of powers of attorney and healthcare directives, providing guidance on how to implement them effectively.

Powers of Attorney

Powers of attorney are legal documents that designate an agent to make decisions on your behalf. They provide a framework for managing your affairs when you are unable to do so yourself.

Types of Powers of Attorney

General Power of Attorney: This document grants broad authority to the agent to manage all aspects of your financial and legal affairs. It can include managing bank accounts, paying bills, buying or selling property, and making investment decisions.

Limited Power of Attorney: A limited power of attorney grants specific, limited powers to the agent for a particular task or period. For example, it might authorize an agent to complete a real estate transaction on your behalf.

Durable Power of Attorney: A durable power of attorney remains in effect even if you become incapacitated, ensuring that your agent can continue to manage your affairs without interruption.

Springing Power of Attorney: A springing power of attorney becomes effective only upon the occurrence of a specific event, such as your incapacitation. This type allows you to maintain control over your affairs until you are unable to manage them.

Choosing an Agent

Trustworthiness: Select an agent who is trustworthy, responsible, and capable of making sound decisions in your best interest. Consider their ability to handle financial matters and manage complex situations.

Communication: Ensure that your chosen agent is willing to communicate openly with you and your family members about decisions and actions taken on your behalf.

Backup Agents: Consider naming a successor or alternate agents in case your primary choice is unable or unwilling to serve. This ensures continuity in decision-making if circumstances change.

Drafting and Executing the Document

Legal Requirements: Work with an experienced attorney to draft the power of attorney document, ensuring it meets state legal requirements and accurately reflects your intentions.

Execution and Storage: Execute the document according to state laws, which typically involve signing it in the presence of a notary and witnesses. Store the document in a safe, accessible location and provide copies to your agent and trusted family members.

Healthcare Directives

Healthcare directives, also known as advance directives, outline your preferences for medical treatment if you are unable to communicate your wishes. They ensure that healthcare providers and loved ones understand your values and treatment preferences.

Types of Healthcare Directives

Living Will: A living will specify the types of medical treatments and life-sustaining measures you want or do not want if you become incapacitated. It can include preferences regarding resuscitation, mechanical ventilation, tube feeding, and palliative care.

Healthcare Power of Attorney: This document designates an agent to make healthcare decisions on your behalf if you are unable to do so. The agent ensures that your medical treatment aligns with your values and wishes.

Do Not Resuscitate (DNR) Order: A DNR order instructs healthcare providers not to perform CPR or other life-saving measures if your heart stops or you stop breathing. It is a critical component of end-of-life planning.

Choosing a Healthcare Agent

Alignment with Values: Choose a healthcare agent who understands and respects your values and beliefs about medical treatment. The agent should be willing and able to advocate for your preferences in challenging situations.

Communication Skills: Select someone who can communicate effectively with healthcare providers and family members, ensuring that your wishes are clearly conveyed and respected.

Backup Agents: Consider naming alternate healthcare agents in case your primary choice is unavailable or unable to serve. This provides flexibility and ensures that someone is always available to make decisions on your behalf.

Discussing Your Wishes

Family Conversations: Engage in open conversations with your family members about your healthcare preferences and the contents of your directives. This helps ensure that everyone understands your wishes and reduces the likelihood of conflicts or misunderstandings.

Communicating with Healthcare Providers: Share copies of your healthcare directives with your doctors and healthcare providers, ensuring that your medical records reflect your preferences.

Reviewing and Updating Directives

Regular Reviews: Regularly review and update your healthcare directives to ensure they remain aligned with your current wishes and any changes in your health or personal circumstances.

Legal Compliance: Ensure that your directives comply with state laws and reflect any changes in legislation or healthcare practices.

Integration with Other Estate Planning Tools

Complementing Wills and Trusts

Unified Planning: Powers of attorney and healthcare directives complement wills and trusts by providing a comprehensive framework for managing both financial and medical decisions.

Coordinated Documents: Ensure that all estate planning documents are coordinated and reflect a unified strategy for managing your affairs. This coordination reduces the risk of conflicts and ensures that all aspects of your estate plan work together seamlessly.

Ensuring Consistency

Avoiding Conflicts: Review all documents to ensure consistency in terms and intentions. Conflicting provisions can lead to confusion and disputes, undermining the effectiveness of your estate plan.

Communicating with Advisors: Work closely with legal, financial, and healthcare advisors to ensure that all elements of your estate plan are consistent and aligned with your overall goals.

By incorporating powers of attorney and healthcare directives into your estate plan, you can ensure that your financial and medical decisions are made according to your wishes, even if you become unable to communicate them. These documents provide peace of mind and protect your interests, offering a comprehensive approach to estate planning that addresses all aspects of your personal and financial affairs.

9.3 Tax Considerations in Estate Planning

Tax efficiency is a critical component of estate planning, as it can significantly impact the value of the assets passed on to beneficiaries. By incorporating strategies to minimize estate, gift, and income taxes, you can preserve more of your wealth for your heirs and ensure that your estate plan aligns with your financial goals. This section explores key tax considerations and strategies for achieving tax-efficient estate planning.

Understanding Estate Taxes

Estate taxes are levied on the transfer of an individual's assets upon death. Understanding how these taxes work and planning accordingly can help reduce the tax burden on your estate.

Federal Estate Tax

Exemption Amount: The federal estate tax is subject to an exemption amount, which allows individuals to transfer a certain value of assets tax-free. Any assets above this threshold are subject to federal estate tax at a rate that can reach up to 40%.

Unified Credit: The federal estate tax exemption is unified with the gift tax exemption, meaning that lifetime gifts reduce the available estate tax exemption. Strategic use of the unified credit can minimize taxes and maximize wealth transfer.

State Estate Taxes

State Variations: Some states impose their own estate taxes with different exemption amounts and rates than the federal government. Understanding your state's estate tax laws is essential for comprehensive planning.

State-Specific Strategies: Implementing strategies such as making lifetime gifts or establishing trusts can help reduce state estate taxes and preserve more of your estate for beneficiaries.

Gift Taxes and Strategies

Gift taxes apply to the transfer of assets during an individual's lifetime. Proper planning can leverage gift tax exemptions and reduce overall tax liability.

Annual Gift Tax Exclusion

Exclusion Amount: The annual gift tax exclusion allows individuals to give a specified amount to each recipient tax-free each year. For 2024, this amount is $17,000 per recipient.

Leveraging Exclusions: Making annual gifts within the exclusion limit can reduce the size of your taxable estate and allow you to transfer wealth to heirs gradually.

Lifetime Gift Tax Exemption

Unified Exemption: The lifetime gift tax exemption is unified with the estate tax exemption. Strategic use of this exemption allows for significant tax-free transfers during your lifetime.

Reducing Estate Size: By using the lifetime gift tax exemption, you can reduce the size of your estate and the associated tax liability, allowing for more efficient wealth transfer.

Gifting Strategies

Direct Gifts: Direct gifts to beneficiaries reduce the value of your estate and utilize the annual gift tax exclusion.

Education and Medical Payments: Payments made directly to educational institutions or medical providers on behalf of another person are not subject to gift tax and do not count against the annual exclusion.

Family Limited Partnerships (FLPs): Establishing FLPs allows for the transfer of business interests at a discounted value, providing tax advantages while retaining control over the business.

Income Taxes in Estate Planning

Income taxes can affect both the estate and the beneficiaries. Understanding the impact of income taxes and implementing strategies to minimize them is essential.

Step-Up in Basis

Capital Gains Tax: When an asset is inherited, its cost basis is typically "stepped up" to its fair market value at the time of the owner's death. This step-up in basis reduces capital gains taxes if the asset is later sold.

Maximizing Benefits: Properly identifying assets that benefit from a step-up in basis can minimize capital gains taxes for heirs and enhance the overall tax efficiency of the estate plan.

Trust Income Taxes

Taxation of Trust Income: Trusts are subject to their own tax rates, which can be higher than individual rates. Properly managing distributions and timing can help minimize taxes.

Distribution Planning: Distributing trust income to beneficiaries, who may be in lower tax brackets, can reduce the overall tax liability of the trust.

Charitable Giving as a Tax Strategy

Incorporating charitable giving into your estate plan can provide significant tax benefits while supporting causes you care about.

Charitable Remainder Trusts (CRTs)

Income Stream and Tax Benefits: A CRT provides income to the grantor or other beneficiaries for a set period, with the remainder going to charity. It offers income tax deductions and can help reduce estate taxes.

Avoiding Capital Gains: Transferring appreciated assets to a CRT allows for their sale without incurring capital gains taxes, maximizing the value of the gift.

Charitable Lead Trusts (CLTs)

Immediate Charitable Impact: A CLT provides income to a charity for a set period, after which the remaining assets are transferred to heirs. It can reduce gift and estate taxes, allowing for more tax-efficient transfers to beneficiaries.

Donor-Advised Funds (DAFs)

Flexible Giving: DAFs allow individuals to make charitable contributions, receive immediate tax deductions, and recommend grants to charities over time. They offer flexibility in managing philanthropic goals while providing tax benefits.

Trusts as Tax Planning Tools

Trusts are versatile estate planning tools that can provide tax advantages and enhance the efficiency of wealth transfer.

Irrevocable Life Insurance Trusts (ILITs)

Excluding Insurance Proceeds: An ILIT holds life insurance policies outside of the taxable estate, ensuring that the death benefit is not subject to estate taxes.

Funding the Trust: Premiums can be paid through annual gifts, using the gift tax exclusion to fund the trust without incurring gift taxes.

Grantor Retained Annuity Trusts (GRATs)

Transferring Appreciation: A GRAT allows for the transfer of asset appreciation to beneficiaries with minimal gift tax implications. The grantor retains an annuity for a specified term, with any remaining assets passing to beneficiaries tax-free.

Low-Interest Environment: GRATs are particularly effective in low-interest-rate environments, allowing for greater potential transfer of wealth.

Dynasty Trusts

Preserving Wealth Across Generations: Dynasty trusts are designed to last for multiple generations, providing tax-efficient wealth transfer while minimizing estate taxes through successive generations.

Leveraging Exemptions: Proper use of generation-skipping transfer tax exemptions can enhance the tax efficiency of dynasty trusts.

By understanding and implementing these tax considerations and strategies, you can create a comprehensive and tax-efficient estate plan that maximizes the value of your assets and preserves wealth for future generations. Collaborating with experienced tax and legal professionals ensures that your estate plan is tailored to your unique circumstances and optimizes tax savings while achieving your financial goals.

Chapter 10: Digital Estate Planning

In today's digital age, digital assets have become an integral part of personal and financial affairs. From online banking and investment accounts to social media profiles and digital photo collections, these assets hold significant value and importance. Digital estate planning is the process of organizing, managing, and transferring digital assets as part of your comprehensive estate plan. This chapter explores the importance of digital estate planning, the types of digital assets to consider, and the steps to effectively incorporate them into your estate plan.

The Importance of Digital Estate Planning

As digital assets continue to grow in significance, it is essential to include them in your estate planning process. Failing to plan for these assets can lead to loss of value, identity theft, and challenges for your heirs. Here are some reasons why digital estate planning is crucial:

Preservation of Value: Digital assets, such as cryptocurrency and online investment accounts, can hold substantial financial value. Ensuring that these assets are accessible and transferable can prevent financial loss for your heirs.

Protection of Personal Information: Many digital accounts contain sensitive personal information that must be protected from unauthorized access. Proper planning helps safeguard your digital identity and prevents identity theft.

Continuation of Online Presence: Social media profiles and personal websites are extensions of your identity and can continue to impact your reputation after your passing. Planning for these accounts ensures they are managed according to your wishes.

Emotional Significance: Digital photos, videos, and documents often hold sentimental value for your loved ones. Proper planning allows these assets to be preserved and shared with family members.

Types of Digital Assets to Consider

Digital assets encompass a wide range of online and electronic properties. When creating your digital estate plan, consider the following types of assets:

Financial Accounts

- **Online Banking:** Accounts used for managing personal and business finances.
- **Investment Platforms**: Accounts used for trading stocks, bonds, and other securities.
- **Cryptocurrency Wallets**: Digital wallets used to store, manage, and transfer cryptocurrencies like Bitcoin and Ethereum.

Social Media and Online Presence

- **Social Media Accounts:** Profiles on platforms such as Facebook, Twitter, Instagram, and LinkedIn.
- **Personal Blogs and Websites:** Sites you own or manage, which may contain personal or professional content.

Email and Communication Accounts

- **Email Accounts:** Platforms used for personal and professional correspondence.
- **Messaging Apps**: Services like WhatsApp, Messenger, and Telegram.

Digital Media and Content

- **Photo and Video Libraries**: Collections stored on platforms like Google Photos, iCloud, and Dropbox.
- **Music and eBook Libraries**: Purchased content stored on platforms like iTunes, Amazon Kindle, and Spotify.

Online Subscriptions and Services

- **Streaming Services:** Accounts with services like Netflix, Hulu, and Disney+.
- **Cloud Storage:** Accounts with providers like Google Drive and OneDrive.

Business Accounts and Platforms

- **Domain Names:** Registered domains used for personal or business websites.

- **E-commerce Accounts:** Platforms used for online sales and transactions, such as Etsy, eBay, or Shopify.

Steps for Effective Digital Estate Planning

To ensure that your digital assets are properly managed and transferred, follow these steps to create an effective digital estate plan:

Inventory Your Digital Assets

- **Comprehensive Listing**: Create a detailed inventory of all your digital assets, including account names, URLs, and login information. This list should encompass financial accounts, social media profiles, email accounts, and other digital properties.
- **Update Regularly:** Keep the inventory updated to reflect any changes in accounts or new digital assets acquired over time.

Securely Store Access Information

- **Password Management**: Use a secure password manager to store login credentials and security information for all digital accounts. This ensures that your executor or designated agent can access your accounts when necessary.
- **Encryption and Security**: Protect sensitive information with strong encryption and security measures to prevent unauthorized access.

Designate a Digital Executor

- **Role and Responsibilities**: Appoint a digital executor who is responsible for managing and distributing your digital assets according to your wishes. This individual should be tech-savvy and familiar with your digital landscape.
- **Legal Authority:** Ensure that the digital executor has the legal authority to access and manage your digital assets by including specific provisions in your will or trust documents.

Create a Digital Estate Plan

- **Incorporate into Existing Plan**: Integrate digital asset management into your overall estate plan by including specific instructions for handling these assets in your will or trust.
- **Provide Clear Instructions:** Outline your wishes for each type of digital asset, including whether accounts should be deleted, transferred, or memorialized.

Address Legal and Privacy Issues

- **Terms of Service Agreements**: Review the terms of service agreements for each digital account to understand the legal implications of transferring or accessing these assets.
- **Data Privacy:** Ensure that your digital estate plan complies with relevant data privacy laws and regulations to protect your personal information.

Communicate with Loved Ones

- **Inform Family Members: Discuss** your digital estate plan with family members and ensure that your designated digital executor is aware of their responsibilities.
- **Share Access Information:** Provide trusted individuals with access to your password manager or other secure methods for accessing your digital assets.

Review and Update Regularly

- **Ongoing Review:** Periodically review your digital estate plan to ensure it remains current and reflects any changes in your digital assets or personal wishes.
- **Stay Informed:** Keep up to date with changes in technology and digital estate planning best practices to ensure your plan remains effective.

By incorporating digital assets into your estate plan, you can ensure that your online and electronic properties are managed according to your wishes and that their value is preserved for your heirs. Digital estate planning provides peace of mind and protects your digital legacy, ensuring that your personal and financial affairs are handled smoothly in the digital realm.

10.1 Managing Digital Assets: Best Practices for Organization and Security

As digital assets become increasingly important in our lives, managing them effectively is crucial for both personal convenience and estate planning. Proper organization and security measures ensure that these assets are accessible, protected, and transferable to your heirs. This section outlines best practices for managing digital assets, focusing on organization and security strategies.

Organizing Digital Assets

Create a Comprehensive Inventory

Identify All Digital Assets: Start by listing all your digital assets, including financial accounts, social media profiles, email accounts, and digital media. Be thorough in capturing both the assets' nature and their purpose.

Categorize Assets: Organize assets into categories such as financial, personal, and business. This categorization makes it easier to manage and prioritize assets based on their significance and usage.

Include Key Details: For each asset, record important details such as account numbers, URLs, usernames, passwords, and security questions. Also, note any recurring payments or subscriptions associated with each account.

Regularly Update the Inventory

Review and Revise: Schedule regular reviews of your digital asset inventory to ensure it remains up to date. Add new accounts, remove inactive ones, and update any changes in login credentials or security settings.

Track Changes: Keep a record of changes made to your digital assets, such as password updates, new account registrations, or changes in service terms. This helps maintain an accurate overview of your digital landscape.

Use a Centralized System for Management

Digital Asset Management Tools: Consider using digital asset management tools or software to help organize and track your assets. These tools offer features like tagging, categorization, and search capabilities, making it easier to manage complex digital estates.

Spreadsheets and Documents: Alternatively, use spreadsheets or documents to maintain your inventory, ensuring they are securely stored and accessible only to trusted individuals.

Prioritize Important Assets

Identify High-Priority Assets: Determine which digital assets hold the most value or importance, such as financial accounts, business-related assets, or personal files with sentimental value.

Focus on Key Accounts: Ensure that high-priority accounts are accurately documented and regularly monitored for security and access issues.

Securing Digital Assets

Use Strong Passwords

Create Unique Passwords: Use unique, complex passwords for each digital account. Avoid using easily guessable information such as birthdays, names, or common words.

Password Length and Complexity: Aim for passwords that are at least 12 characters long, combining uppercase and lowercase letters, numbers, and symbols for added security.

Implement Two-Factor Authentication (2FA)

Enhanced Security: Enable two-factor authentication for accounts that support it. 2FA adds an extra layer of security by requiring a second verification step, such as a text message code or authentication app, in addition to your password.

Regularly Update 2FA Methods: Periodically review and update your 2FA settings to ensure they remain effective and aligned with the latest security practices.

Use a Password Manager

Secure Storage: Utilize a password manager to securely store and manage your login credentials. Password managers generate and store strong passwords, reducing the risk of unauthorized access.

Access Control: Ensure that your password manager is protected with a strong master password and, if available, two-factor authentication.

Back Up Important Data

Regular Backups: Perform regular backups of important digital files, such as documents, photos, and videos, to protect against data loss due to hardware failure, accidental deletion, or cyberattacks.

Cloud and Physical Storage: Use a combination of cloud-based and physical storage solutions (e.g., external hard drives) to ensure data redundancy and accessibility.

Monitor Account Activity

Regular Checks: Regularly monitor account activity for signs of unauthorized access or suspicious behaviour. Promptly address any security alerts or unusual transactions.

Alerts and Notifications: Enable alerts and notifications for account activities, such as login attempts, password changes, or financial transactions, to stay informed about any changes or potential security breaches.

Stay Informed About Security Risks

Cybersecurity Awareness: Stay informed about the latest cybersecurity threats and best practices. Educate yourself about common scams, phishing attacks, and other online risks to protect your digital assets.

Security Updates: Keep your devices and software updated with the latest security patches and updates to protect against vulnerabilities.

Sharing Access with Trusted Individuals

Designate a Digital Executor

Legal Authority: Appoint a digital executor in your estate plan who has the authority to manage and transfer your digital assets according to your wishes. This person should be familiar with your digital landscape and capable of handling the responsibilities.

Clear Instructions: Provide clear instructions to your digital executor regarding your preferences for managing and distributing digital assets.

Share Access Information Securely

Limited Access: Share access information for critical accounts only with trusted individuals, such as your digital executor or close family members.

Secure Communication: Use secure methods to share access information, such as encrypted emails or secure file-sharing services, to prevent unauthorized access.

Establish Contingency Plans

Successor Plans: Designate alternate individuals who can step in if your primary digital executor is unable or unwilling to serve.

Emergency Access: Consider creating an emergency access plan that provides specific instructions for accessing critical accounts in urgent situations.

By implementing these best practices for organizing and securing digital assets, you can ensure that your digital estate is managed efficiently and protected against unauthorized access. Proper management and security of digital assets provide peace of mind and facilitate a seamless transition of these assets to your heirs, preserving their value and significance.

10.2 Planning for Social Media and Online Accounts

Social media platforms and online accounts have become integral to personal and professional life, representing a significant portion of our digital identity and presence. Properly managing these accounts in the context of estate planning ensures that they are handled according to your wishes, whether you want them memorialized, deleted, or transferred. This section explores best practices for planning the future of your social media and online accounts.

Understanding the Impact of Social Media and Online Accounts

Digital Legacy

Personal Expression: Social media accounts are often used for personal expression, sharing milestones, and documenting important life events. These platforms can carry sentimental value for both the account holder and their loved ones.

Professional Reputation: For many, social media and online accounts are tied to their professional reputation and personal brand, influencing career opportunities and professional relationships.

Privacy and Security Concerns

Sensitive Information: Online accounts may contain sensitive personal information that could be vulnerable to unauthorized access if not managed properly.

Potential for Misuse: Without proper planning, social media accounts could be subject to misuse, identity theft, or fraudulent activity.

Steps for Planning Social Media and Online Accounts

Inventory Your Online Accounts

Comprehensive List: Create an inventory of all your social media and online accounts, including platforms like Facebook, Twitter, Instagram, LinkedIn, and personal blogs.

Account Details: Record account information, including usernames, passwords, and security settings. Include any associated accounts or services linked to each platform.

Determine Your Preferences

Account Management: Decide how you want each account to be managed after your passing. Options include memorialization, deletion, or transfer to a designated individual.

Specific Instructions: Provide specific instructions for each account, detailing how you wish to handle posts, messages, photos, and other content.

Review Platform Policies

Terms of Service: Familiarize yourself with the terms of service and policies of each platform regarding account management after death. Some platforms offer specific options, such as memorializing or deactivating accounts.

Access and Control: Understand the requirements for gaining access to or managing an account after the owner's death. This may involve providing documentation or proof of authority.

Designate a Digital Executor

Role and Authority: Appoint a digital executor in your estate plan who is responsible for managing your social media and online accounts according to your wishes.

Clear Instructions: Provide clear instructions and authority to your digital executor, ensuring they understand their responsibilities and have the necessary access information.

Communicate with Loved Ones

Discuss Your Wishes: Share your plans for social media and online accounts with trusted family members or friends. Open communication ensures that your loved ones understand your preferences and can support your digital executor.

Address Concerns: Discuss any specific concerns or sentimental attachments to your online presence, providing guidance on how you want them to be addressed.

Managing Different Types of Accounts

Social Media Platforms

Memorialization: Some platforms, like Facebook, offer a memorialization option, allowing accounts to remain active as a digital legacy for friends and family to visit and remember. Determine if this aligns with your wishes.

Account Deactivation: If you prefer to close accounts, instruct your digital executor to deactivate or delete them, following the platform's procedures.

Professional Networks

LinkedIn: For professional networks like LinkedIn, consider how you want your profile managed. You may wish to inform professional contacts or provide a farewell message.

Portfolio Sites: If you have personal websites or portfolios, provide instructions for their management or closure.

Personal Blogs and Websites

Content Preservation: If you wish to preserve content from personal blogs or websites, instruct your digital executor to archive or transfer the content to a trusted individual or family member.

Domain Management: Provide instructions for managing domain names, including whether they should be renewed, transferred, or allowed to expire.

Security Considerations

Account Security

Password Management: Use a password manager to store and manage login credentials for all online accounts. Ensure your digital executor has secure access to this information.

Two-Factor Authentication: Enable two-factor authentication (2FA) for accounts that support it, enhancing security and protecting against unauthorized access.

Data Privacy

Protect Sensitive Information: Ensure that sensitive personal information within accounts is protected and instruct your digital executor on how to handle it securely.

Monitor for Activity: Instruct your digital executor to monitor accounts for suspicious activity or unauthorized access, taking appropriate action if necessary.

Legal and Ethical Considerations

Legal Authority

Incorporate into Estate Plan: Include provisions for managing social media and online accounts in your will or trust documents, ensuring your digital executor has the legal authority to act.

Compliance with Laws: Ensure that your digital estate plan complies with applicable data privacy laws and regulations, protecting your rights and the rights of your heirs.

Ethical Considerations

Respecting Privacy: Consider the privacy of other individuals involved in your online interactions and provide guidance on how to handle content that may affect others.

Honouring Intentions: Ensure that your digital executor understands and respects your intentions, managing your digital legacy with care and integrity.

By proactively planning for your social media and online accounts, you can ensure that your digital presence is managed according to your wishes and that its value and significance are preserved for your loved ones. Proper management of these accounts safeguards your digital legacy, providing peace of mind and continuity for both personal and professional aspects of your life.

10.3 Cryptocurrency and Digital Assets: Incorporating Modern Investments into Estate Planning

Cryptocurrencies and digital assets have emerged as significant components of modern investment portfolios. As their popularity and value increase, it is essential to incorporate these assets into your estate plan. Properly managing and transferring cryptocurrency requires unique considerations due to their decentralized nature and security requirements. This section explores the best practices for including cryptocurrency and other digital assets in your estate plan.

Understanding Cryptocurrency and Digital Assets

What is Cryptocurrency?

Decentralized Currency: Cryptocurrency is a form of digital currency that uses cryptography for security and operates on a decentralized network called blockchain. Popular cryptocurrencies include Bitcoin, Ethereum, and Litecoin.

Volatility and Value: Cryptocurrencies are known for their price volatility and potential for high returns. Their value can fluctuate significantly, impacting estate planning strategies.

Other Digital Assets

Non-Fungible Tokens (NFTs): NFTs are unique digital assets that represent ownership of specific digital items, such as art, music, or collectibles. They are stored on blockchain networks and can hold substantial value.

Digital Collectibles and Virtual Real Estate: Digital assets also include virtual real estate in online worlds or digital collectibles in games, which can be bought, sold, and traded.

Challenges of Incorporating Cryptocurrency into Estate Planning

Complex Access and Security

Private Keys: Cryptocurrency ownership is determined by access to private keys, which are crucial for authorizing transactions. Losing these keys means losing access to the cryptocurrency.

Security Risks: Digital assets are susceptible to cyberattacks and theft, requiring robust security measures to protect them.

Lack of Regulation and Clarity

Regulatory Environment: The regulatory landscape for cryptocurrencies is still evolving, leading to uncertainties in estate planning and tax implications.

Legal Considerations: Traditional legal frameworks may not fully address the unique characteristics of digital assets, posing challenges in estate administration.

Volatility and Valuation

Fluctuating Value: The volatile nature of cryptocurrencies can complicate estate planning, affecting the overall value of the estate and distribution strategies.

Valuation Methods: Determining the fair market value of digital assets for estate and tax purposes can be complex, especially for less liquid or newly created assets.

Best Practices for Including Cryptocurrency in Estate Planning

Document and Inventory Digital Assets

Comprehensive Listing: Create a detailed inventory of all your digital assets, including cryptocurrencies, NFTs, and any other digital holdings. Include information about where they are stored and how they can be accessed.

Update Regularly: Keep your inventory up to date, reflecting changes in holdings, values, and storage locations.

Secure Access Information

Private Key Management: Safely store private keys and access information in a secure, encrypted manner. Consider using a hardware wallet or a reputable password manager to store this sensitive data.

Backup and Redundancy: Create secure backups of private keys and access information to prevent loss due to device failure or accidental deletion.

Designate a Digital Executor

Appoint a Knowledgeable Executor: Choose a digital executor who understands cryptocurrencies and has the technical expertise to manage these assets. Ensure they have the legal authority to access and transfer your digital holdings.

Provide Clear Instructions: Outline specific instructions for managing and transferring digital assets, including how to access and distribute them according to your wishes.

Integrate Digital Assets into Estate Documents

Include in Wills and Trusts: Ensure that digital assets are included in your will or trust documents, specifying how they should be managed and distributed. Consider using specific language that addresses the unique nature of these assets.

Address Legal and Tax Considerations: Work with legal and tax professionals to address any regulatory and tax implications of digital assets. Ensure that your estate plan complies with applicable laws and takes advantage of available tax strategies.

Consider Tax Implications

Capital Gains and Income Tax: Understand the tax implications of cryptocurrency transactions, including capital gains and income tax considerations. Proper planning can help minimize tax liabilities and optimize wealth transfer.

Gifting and Donation Strategies: Explore gifting or donating digital assets as part of your estate plan to reduce the taxable estate and support charitable causes.

Stay Informed and Adapt

Monitor Regulatory Changes: Stay informed about changes in cryptocurrency regulations and estate planning practices to ensure your plan remains current and compliant.

Review and Update Regularly: Periodically review and update your estate plan to reflect changes in digital asset holdings, values, and legal environments.

Security Measures for Digital Assets

Use Secure Storage Solutions

Hardware Wallets: Consider using hardware wallets to store private keys offline, providing a high level of security against cyber threats.

Cold Storage: Utilize cold storage solutions for long-term storage of digital assets, reducing exposure to online vulnerabilities.

Implement Robust Cybersecurity Practices

Strong Passwords and 2FA: Use strong passwords and enable two-factor authentication (2FA) for accounts associated with digital assets.

Regular Security Audits: Conduct regular security audits of your digital asset storage solutions and practices to identify and mitigate potential risks.

Plan for Access in Emergencies

Emergency Access Plan: Develop an emergency access plan that provides instructions for accessing digital assets in case of sudden incapacitation or death.

Trusted Contacts: Designate trusted contacts who can assist with accessing and managing digital assets in emergencies.

By effectively managing and incorporating cryptocurrencies and digital assets into your estate plan, you can ensure that these modern investments are protected, accessible, and transferable according to your wishes. Proper planning and security measures provide peace of mind, safeguarding the value and integrity of your digital assets for future generations.

Chapter 11: Family Dynamics and Communication in Estate Planning

Estate planning is not just about legal documents and financial strategies; it also involves addressing the human element—family dynamics and effective communication. Navigating the complexities of family relationships and ensuring that your wishes are clearly understood can significantly impact the success of your estate plan. This chapter explores how to manage family dynamics and foster open communication to ensure a smooth estate planning process.

Understanding Family Dynamics

Identifying Key Relationships

Nuclear Family: Consider the roles and relationships within your immediate family, including spouses, children, and stepchildren. These relationships are often central to estate planning decisions.

Extended Family: Evaluate relationships with extended family members, such as siblings, parents, and in-laws, who may also be affected by your estate plan.

Blended Families: Address the complexities of blended families, where multiple sets of children or step-relatives may have competing interests or expectations.

Recognizing Potential Conflicts

Inheritance Disparities: Differences in inheritance allocations can lead to disputes or feelings of resentment among family members. Anticipate these issues and plan accordingly.

Family Business Succession: In families with a business, succession planning can be a source of tension, especially when some members are involved in the business and others are not.

Caretaking Responsibilities: Decisions about caretaking for elderly or disabled family members can create conflict, particularly if certain members feel overburdened or underappreciated.

Balancing Fairness and Equality

Perceptions of Fairness: Understand that perceptions of fairness and equality can differ among family members. Communicate the reasoning behind your decisions to manage expectations.

Customized Solutions: Develop customized solutions that reflect the unique needs and contributions of each family member, rather than applying a one-size-fits-all approach.

Effective Communication Strategies

Start Early and Involve Key Players

Proactive Discussions: Initiate conversations about your estate plan early, involving key family members in the process. This fosters transparency and reduces uncertainty.

Inclusive Approach: Include those affected by your estate plan in discussions to ensure that their perspectives are considered and that they understand your intentions.

Clarify Your Intentions

Clear Explanations: Clearly explain the reasoning behind your estate planning decisions, particularly if they deviate from expectations. This clarity helps prevent misunderstandings and resentment.

Documented Wishes: Ensure that your intentions are clearly documented in legal documents, providing a reference point for family members and reducing ambiguity.

Use Family Meetings

Structured Discussions: Organize family meetings to discuss your estate plan and address any questions or concerns. This structured approach allows for open dialogue and collective problem-solving.

Facilitated Conversations: Consider using a professional mediator or estate planner to facilitate discussions, particularly if family dynamics are complex or contentious.

Address Sensitive Topics

Emotional Preparedness: Recognize that estate planning involves sensitive topics, such as mortality, financial disparities, and family roles. Approach these topics with empathy and understanding.

Conflict Resolution: Be prepared to address conflicts and disagreements constructively, seeking solutions that respect the needs and feelings of all parties involved.

Communicate Regularly

Ongoing Dialogue: Maintain an ongoing dialogue about your estate plan, providing updates as circumstances change. Regular communication helps reinforce understanding and trust.

Review and Revise: Periodically review and update your estate plan to reflect changes in family dynamics, relationships, or financial circumstances.

Incorporating Family Values and Legacy

Articulate Your Values

Values Statement: Create a values statement that articulates your core beliefs and priorities. This statement can guide your estate planning decisions and provide a foundation for family discussions.

Legacy Goals: Identify your legacy goals, such as philanthropic endeavours, educational support, or the preservation of family traditions. Communicate these goals to your family and incorporate them into your estate plan.

Foster Family Cohesion

Shared Vision: Encourage a shared vision for the family's future, fostering unity and collaboration in achieving common goals.

Family Mission Statement: Develop a family mission statement that outlines shared values and objectives. This statement can guide decision-making and strengthen family bonds.

Encourage Financial Literacy

Education and Empowerment: Provide financial education to family members, empowering them to make informed decisions and manage their inheritance responsibly.

Successor Preparation: Prepare successors for future roles, particularly in family businesses or philanthropic efforts, through mentorship and training.

Navigating Difficult Conversations

Anticipate Sensitive Issues

Identify Potential Triggers: Recognize issues that may be emotionally charged or contentious, such as disinheritance, unequal distributions, or guardianship decisions.

Plan for Challenges: Develop strategies for addressing these issues, anticipating possible reactions and preparing responses that demonstrate empathy and understanding.

Use Empathy and Active Listening

Empathetic Approach: Approach discussions with empathy, acknowledging the emotions and concerns of family members. Validate their feelings and show understanding.

Active Listening: Practice active listening by giving full attention to the speaker, reflecting on their words, and asking clarifying questions. This fosters mutual respect and open communication.

Seek Professional Guidance

Mediation and Counselling: Engage professional mediators or family counsellors to facilitate difficult conversations and provide impartial guidance in resolving conflicts.

Legal and Financial Advisors: Consult with legal and financial advisors to ensure that your estate plan is well-structured and addresses any potential legal or financial challenges.

By understanding family dynamics and fostering open communication, you can create an estate plan that not only protects your assets but also strengthens family relationships and honours your legacy. A thoughtful approach to estate planning involves balancing legal, financial, and emotional considerations, ensuring that your wishes are respected, and your family's future is secured.

11.1 Navigating Complex Family Structures in Estate Planning

Modern families often have complex structures that can present unique challenges in estate planning. Blended families, multiple marriages, cohabitation without marriage, and extended family dynamics require careful consideration to ensure that your estate plan reflects your wishes and addresses the needs of all family members. This section explores strategies for navigating complex family structures in estate planning.

Blended Families

Blended families, which include children from previous relationships, require thoughtful planning to balance the interests of different family members and prevent potential conflicts.

Clarifying Inheritance Goals

Equal vs. Equitable Distribution: Decide whether your goal is to distribute assets equally among all children or equitably based on individual needs and circumstances. Clearly communicate your reasoning to avoid misunderstandings

Spouse vs. Children: Determine how to balance the inheritance between your current spouse and children from previous relationships. Consider the financial security of your spouse while ensuring that children receive their intended inheritance.

Using Trusts for Flexibility

Qualified Terminable Interest Property (QTIP) Trust: A QTIP trust can provide income for your surviving spouse while preserving the principal for children from a previous marriage. This ensures financial support for your spouse and protects your children's inheritance.

Revocable Living Trust: Establish a revocable living trust to outline specific distributions for each beneficiary. This allows you to retain control and make changes as needed, providing flexibility to adapt to changing family dynamics.

Designating Beneficiaries

Beneficiary Designations: Regularly review and update beneficiary designations on retirement accounts, life insurance policies, and other assets to ensure they align with your estate plan.

Contingent Beneficiaries: Designate contingent beneficiaries to address the possibility that a primary beneficiary may predecease you or decline the inheritance.

Prenuptial and Postnuptial Agreement

Defining Asset Ownership: Use prenuptial or postnuptial agreements to define asset ownership and clarify financial responsibilities within the marriage. These agreements can provide clarity and prevent disputes over inheritance.

Protecting Separate Assets: Specify separate assets that should remain outside the marital estate, ensuring that they are preserved for your intended beneficiaries.

Cohabitation Without Marriage

For couples who choose to cohabit without marriage, it is important to create an estate plan that protects both partners and ensures their wishes are honoured.

Estate Planning Documents

Wills and Trusts: Draft wills and trusts that clearly outline asset distribution and specify your partner as a beneficiary if desired. Without a legal marriage, your partner may not have automatic inheritance rights.

Joint Ownership: Consider joint ownership of assets, such as real estate or bank accounts, to ensure that your partner has access and ownership upon your passing.

Healthcare and Financial Decisions

Powers of Attorney: Execute durable powers of attorney for healthcare and finances, granting your partner the authority to make decisions on your behalf if you become incapacitated.

Healthcare Directives: Include your partner in healthcare directives to ensure they have the authority to participate in medical decisions and access your medical information.

Protecting Each Partner's Interests

Cohabitation Agreement: Draft a cohabitation agreement to clarify financial responsibilities and asset ownership during the relationship. This agreement can help prevent disputes and protect each partner's interests.

Beneficiary Designations: Regularly update beneficiary designations on accounts and policies to reflect your partner's role and ensure they receive intended benefits.

Extended Family Dynamics

Estate planning for extended families, including grandparents, aunts, uncles, and other relatives, requires consideration of their roles and potential contributions to the family's legacy.

Involving Extended Family

Family Meetings: Hold family meetings to discuss estate planning goals and gather input from extended family members. Involving them in the planning process can foster unity and collaboration.

Gifts and Loans: Consider how gifts or loans to extended family members will impact your estate plan. Clearly document any financial arrangements to prevent misunderstandings or disputes.

Grandparent Involvement

Educational Funding: Set up educational trusts or 529 plans to support grandchildren's education. This allows grandparents to contribute to their legacy while providing valuable support.

Inclusion in Estate Plan: Include provisions in your estate plan for extended family members, such as specific bequests or charitable contributions in their honour.

Supporting Elderly Relatives

Caregiving Arrangements: Address caregiving responsibilities for elderly relatives within your estate plan. Consider financial support, living arrangements, and healthcare decisions.

Multi-Generational Planning: Develop a multi-generational estate plan that considers the needs of older and younger generations, fostering a sense of continuity and shared responsibility.

Managing Potential Conflicts

Open Communication

Transparent Discussions: Encourage open and transparent discussions about your estate plan with all family members. Clear communication helps prevent misunderstandings and promotes harmony.

Addressing Concerns: Be receptive to concerns or questions from family members and address them constructively. Providing explanations for your decisions can help mitigate potential conflicts.

Professional Guidance

Engage Advisors: Work with legal, financial, and tax advisors to develop an estate plan that addresses complex family dynamics and aligns with your goals.

Mediation Services: Consider using mediation services to resolve disputes or disagreements among family members. A neutral third party can facilitate productive conversations and identify solutions.

Regular Review and Updates

Periodic Revisions: Regularly review and update your estate plan to reflect changes in family dynamics, relationships, or financial circumstances.

Adapting to Change: Be open to adapting your estate plan as family relationships evolve or new circumstances arise, ensuring it remains relevant and effective.

By recognizing and addressing the complexities of modern family structures, you can create an estate plan that respects your wishes and supports the needs of all family members. Thoughtful planning and effective communication are key to navigating these challenges and fostering harmony within your family

11.2 Effective Communication Strategies for Family Estate Planning

Effective communication is the cornerstone of successful estate planning, especially when navigating complex family dynamics. Transparent, empathetic, and proactive communication can prevent misunderstandings, reduce conflicts, and ensure that your wishes are clearly understood and respected by all family members. This section outlines effective communication strategies to enhance family estate planning.

Building a Foundation of Trust

Establishing Open Dialogue

Early Discussions: Initiate conversations about estate planning early in the process. Discussing your intentions and plans with family members well in advance fosters transparency and trust.

Regular Updates: Keep family members informed about any changes or updates to your estate plan. Regular communication helps maintain transparency and reduces uncertainty.

Creating a Safe Environment

Encouraging Participation: Create an environment where all family members feel comfortable expressing their thoughts, concerns, and questions. Encourage active participation and input from everyone involved.

Respectful Listening: Practice respectful listening by giving each family member the opportunity to share their perspective without interruption. Acknowledge their feelings and validate their concerns.

Facilitating Productive Family Meetings

Planning and Structure

Agenda Setting: Prepare an agenda for family meetings to ensure that discussions stay focused and productive. Share the agenda in advance so that family members can prepare their thoughts and questions.

Time Management: Allocate sufficient time for each topic on the agenda, allowing for thorough discussion without rushing. Consider scheduling multiple meetings if needed to cover all relevant topics.

Choosing a Facilitator

Neutral Party: Consider using a neutral third party, such as a professional mediator or estate planning advisor, to facilitate discussions. A neutral facilitator can help manage emotions and ensure that everyone's voice is heard.

Family Representative: Alternatively, appoint a family member who is respected by all parties to guide the discussion and keep the meeting on track.

Encouraging Open Communication

Inclusive Participation: Encourage all family members to participate in discussions, ensuring that everyone's perspective is considered. Avoid dominating the conversation or dismissing opposing views.

Active Listening Techniques: Practice active listening by focusing on the speaker, asking clarifying questions, and reflecting on what is being said. This approach demonstrates empathy and fosters understanding.

Addressing Sensitive Topics

Recognizing Emotional Triggers

Identifying Sensitive Issues: Anticipate topics that may evoke strong emotions, such as unequal inheritance, remarriage, or care for elderly parents. Plan how to address these issues sensitively.

Preparing Responses: Prepare thoughtful responses to anticipated concerns, focusing on the rationale behind your decisions and the values that guide your estate plan.

Using Empathy and Compassion

Validating Feelings: Acknowledge and validate the emotions and concerns of family members. Show empathy by putting yourself in their shoes and understanding their perspective.

Focusing on Common Goals: Emphasize shared family values and common goals, such as preserving family harmony or supporting future generations. This approach fosters unity and collaboration.

Providing Clear Explanations

Explaining Your Intentions: Clearly explain the reasoning behind your estate planning decisions, particularly if they deviate from expectations. Transparency reduces misunderstandings and resentment.

Documenting Discussions: Consider documenting discussions and decisions in writing to provide a reference for future conversations and to ensure that everyone is on the same page.

Incorporating Professional Guidance

Engaging Estate Planning Advisors

Legal and Financial Expertise: Work with experienced estate planning advisors to ensure that your plan is legally sound and aligns with your financial goals. Advisors can provide valuable insights and recommendations.

Facilitating Communication: Advisors can also help facilitate family discussions by providing objective information and guiding the conversation on technical matters.

Utilizing Mediation Services

Resolving Conflicts: If conflicts arise, consider engaging a professional mediator to help resolve disputes. Mediation provides a structured process for finding mutually acceptable solutions.

Improving Understanding: Mediation can also improve understanding and communication among family members, helping to rebuild trust and strengthen relationships.

Balancing Privacy and Transparency

Deciding What to Share

Confidentiality Considerations: Decide which aspects of your estate plan to share with family members and which to keep confidential. Consider the potential impact of disclosure on family dynamics.

Sharing Relevant Information: Share information that is relevant to each family member's role or interests, ensuring they have the necessary context to understand your decisions.

Managing Expectations

Setting Realistic Expectations: Clearly communicate what family members can expect from the estate plan, including timelines, responsibilities, and potential outcomes. This helps prevent misunderstandings and disappointment.

Clarifying Roles: Clearly define the roles and responsibilities of each family member in the estate plan, such as executors, trustees, or guardians. Ensure that everyone understands their obligations and is willing to fulfil them.

By implementing effective communication strategies, you can create a more inclusive and harmonious estate planning process. Open dialogue, empathy, and professional guidance help build trust and understanding among family members, ensuring that your estate plan reflects your values and meets the needs of all involved.

11.3 Involving the Next Generation in Estate Planning

Involving the next generation in estate planning is crucial for ensuring a smooth transition of wealth, fostering financial responsibility, and preserving family values and legacy. Engaging younger family members early in the process helps prepare them for future responsibilities and empowers them to contribute to the family's long-term goals. This section explores strategies for involving the next generation in estate planning.

Preparing the Next Generation

Educating on Financial Literacy

Financial Education Programs: Enrol younger family members in financial literacy programs that cover topics such as budgeting, investing, and debt management. Understanding these basics lays the foundation for responsible financial behaviour.

Family Workshops: Host family workshops where financial advisors or educators teach practical skills like tax planning, asset management, and the importance of estate planning. These workshops provide an opportunity for learning and discussion.

Discussing Estate Planning Basics

Importance of Planning: Explain the importance of estate planning and how it benefits the family. Highlight how a well-structured estate plan ensures continuity and protection of family assets.

Basic Concepts: Introduce basic estate planning concepts, such as wills, trusts, and powers of attorney, to demystify the process and foster an understanding of its components.

Involving Them in Discussions

Family Meetings: Invite younger family members to family meetings where estate planning is discussed. Encourage them to ask questions and express their opinions, making them feel included and valued.

Clarifying Expectations: Clearly communicate the expectations and roles of each family member in the estate plan. This clarity helps younger members understand their responsibilities and prepare for future roles.

Empowering the Next Generation

Assigning Responsibilities

Advisory Roles: Assign younger family members advisory roles within the family's financial or philanthropic endeavours. This involvement helps them gain practical experience and develop leadership skills.

Committee Participation: Create committees for specific family projects, such as charitable giving or business succession planning, and involve younger members in decision-making.

Encouraging Philanthropy

Family Philanthropy Projects: Engage the next generation in family philanthropy projects, encouraging them to contribute ideas and participate in charitable activities. This involvement fosters a sense of social responsibility and shared values.

Donor-Advised Funds: Set up donor-advised funds where younger family members can recommend grants to charities, allowing them to experience the impact of philanthropy firsthand.

Mentoring and Training

Mentorship Programs: Establish mentorship programs where older family members mentor younger ones, sharing knowledge and experience related to financial management and estate planning.

Formal Training: Provide formal training opportunities, such as internships or workshops, to help younger members develop skills necessary for managing family assets and businesses.

Preserving Family Values and Legacy

Articulating Family Values

Values Statement: Create a family values statement that articulates the core beliefs and principles that guide your family's decisions. Share this statement with younger members to reinforce shared values.

Legacy Goals: Discuss legacy goals with the next generation, emphasizing the importance of preserving family traditions and contributing to the community.

Developing a Family Mission Statement

Collaborative Process: Involve the next generation in developing a family mission statement that outlines long-term goals and aspirations. This collaboration fosters unity and a shared sense of purpose.

Guiding Principles: Use the mission statement as a guiding framework for family decisions and actions, ensuring alignment with shared values and objectives.

Storytelling and Traditions

Sharing Stories: Share stories about the family's history, achievements, and challenges to provide context and inspiration for the next generation. Personal stories help younger members connect with their heritage.

Continuing Traditions: Encourage the continuation of family traditions that reflect your values and culture. These traditions strengthen bonds and create a sense of belonging.

Navigating Challenges and Conflicts

Anticipating Generational Differences

162

Acknowledging Perspectives: Recognize that younger family members may have different perspectives and priorities, influenced by changing social and economic environments.

Open Dialogue: Foster open dialogue where all family members feel comfortable expressing their views and contributing to discussions.

Addressing Potential Conflicts

Conflict Resolution Skills: Equip the next generation with conflict resolution skills to manage disagreements constructively. Encourage respectful communication and collaborative problem-solving.

Professional Mediation: Consider involving professional mediators if conflicts arise, ensuring that disputes are addressed impartially and effectively.

Balancing Tradition and Innovation

Respecting Traditions: Respect the family's traditions while remaining open to new ideas and innovations proposed by younger members. Balance tradition with adaptability to ensure relevance.

Encouraging Innovation: Encourage the next generation to bring fresh perspectives and innovative ideas to the family's endeavours, fostering growth and progress.

By actively involving the next generation in estate planning, you can prepare them for future responsibilities, empower them to contribute to the family's legacy, and ensure the continuity of family values. Engaging younger family members fosters a sense of ownership and responsibility, helping to secure the family's future and preserve its wealth and heritage for generations to come.

Chapter 12: Legal and Financial Considerations in Estate Planning

Estate planning involves navigating a complex landscape of legal and financial considerations to ensure that your assets are protected, your wishes are honoured, and your beneficiaries are provided for. Understanding these considerations is crucial for creating an effective and legally sound estate plan. This chapter explores the key legal and financial elements involved in estate planning and offers strategies to address them.

Legal Considerations

Estate Planning Documents

Wills: A will is a foundational document that outlines how your assets will be distributed after your death. It allows you to appoint an executor to oversee your estate and designate guardians for minor children. To ensure its validity, your will must comply with state laws regarding execution and witnessing.

Trusts: Trusts are versatile tools that offer privacy, probate avoidance, and asset protection. There are various types of trusts, including revocable, irrevocable, and special purpose trusts, each serving different objectives. Trusts require careful drafting to ensure they align with your goals and legal requirements.

Powers of Attorney: Powers of attorney grant authority to a designated individual to make financial or healthcare decisions on your behalf if you become incapacitated. These documents must clearly outline the scope of authority and include provisions for activation and termination.

Advance Healthcare Directives: Advance directives, including living wills and healthcare proxies, specify your preferences for medical treatment and appoint a representative to make healthcare decisions if you are unable to do so.

Probate and Estate Administration

Probate Process: Probate is the court-supervised process of validating a will, settling debts, and distributing assets to beneficiaries. While it provides legal oversight, probate can be time-consuming and costly, which is why many estate plans aim to minimize or avoid it through trusts and other mechanisms.

Executor Responsibilities: The executor is responsible for managing the estate during probate, including filing necessary paperwork, paying debts and taxes, and distributing assets according to the will. Choosing a reliable and capable executor is essential for efficient estate administration.

Legal Compliance

State Laws: Estate planning laws vary by state, affecting everything from probate procedures to the recognition of certain documents. Ensure your estate plan complies with the laws of your state of residence and consider the implications of owning property in multiple states.

Updates and Revisions: Regularly review and update your estate plan to reflect changes in laws, family circumstances, and financial situations. An outdated estate plan may not accurately reflect your current wishes or be legally enforceable.

Financial Considerations

Asset Management and Distribution

Inventory of Assets: Create a comprehensive inventory of your assets, including real estate, investments, retirement accounts, and personal property. Understanding the full scope of your estate is crucial for effective planning and distribution.

Beneficiary Designations: Ensure beneficiary designations on accounts such as retirement plans, and life insurance policies are up-to-date and align with your estate plan. These designations override instructions in your will, so consistency is key.

Tax Planning

Estate Taxes: Federal and state estate taxes can significantly impact the value of your estate. Implement strategies to minimize taxes, such as taking advantage of lifetime exemptions, gifting, and establishing tax-efficient trusts.

Gift and Income Taxes: Consider the tax implications of lifetime gifts and the impact of income taxes on your beneficiaries. Gifting strategies and trust structures can help mitigate these tax burdens and maximize the transfer of wealth.

Business Succession Planning

Continuity Planning: For business owners, succession planning is critical to ensure the continued operation and success of the business after your passing. Develop a succession plan that outline leadership transitions, ownership transfers, and operational continuity.

Valuation and Transfer: Regularly assess the value of your business interests and determine the most tax-efficient method of transferring ownership, whether through a sale, gift, or trust.

Charitable Giving

Philanthropic Goals: Incorporate charitable giving into your estate plan to support causes you care about and achieve tax benefits. Options include charitable trusts, donor-advised funds, and bequests.

Impact Assessment: Consider the impact of your charitable contributions on your overall estate plan and financial goals. Ensure that your giving aligns with your legacy and values.

Risk Management and Protection

Asset Protection Strategies

Trust Structures: Use trusts to protect assets from creditors and legal claims, particularly in professions with high liability risks. Irrevocable trusts and asset protection trusts can offer significant security.

Insurance Coverage: Ensure you have adequate insurance coverage, including life, health, disability, and liability insurance, to protect your estate and provide for your beneficiaries.

Planning for Incapacity

Long-Term Care Planning: Address the potential need for long-term care and its financial implications. Consider long-term care insurance or Medicaid planning to cover these costs without depleting your estate.

Incapacity Documents: Ensure you have durable powers of attorney and healthcare directives in place to manage your affairs if you become incapacitated. These documents provide peace of mind and continuity in decision-making.

Contingency Planning

Emergency Plans: Develop contingency plans for unexpected events, such as sudden illness or financial setbacks. Having a clear plan in place ensures your estate remains secure and your family is protected.

Successor Designations: Designate successors for key roles, such as trustees or executors, to ensure a seamless transition and continuity in estate management.

Navigating the legal and financial considerations of estate planning requires a comprehensive understanding of both the technical aspects and the personal goals that drive your plan. By working with experienced legal and financial advisors, you can create a robust estate plan that addresses these considerations, protects your assets, and provides for your loved ones. Thoughtful planning and proactive management of your estate ensure that your wishes are honoured and your legacy is preserved for future generations.

12.1 Navigating Estate Taxes: Strategies for Minimizing the Tax Burden

Estate taxes can significantly impact the value of the assets you pass on to your heirs, making tax planning an essential component of a comprehensive estate plan. By understanding the various tax implications and implementing strategic measures, you can minimize the tax burden on your estate and preserve more wealth for your beneficiaries. This section explores effective strategies for navigating estate taxes.

Understanding Estate Taxes

Federal Estate Tax

Exemption Amount: The federal estate tax applies to the transfer of assets upon death. As of 2024, the federal estate tax exemption is $12.92 million per individual, meaning that estates valued below this amount are not subject to federal estate taxes. For married couples, the exemption can be doubled through portability.

Tax Rates: For estates exceeding the exemption threshold, the tax rate can be as high as 40%. Proper planning can help reduce the taxable estate and mitigate these costs.

State Estate Taxes

State Variations: Some states impose their own estate or inheritance taxes, with exemption amounts and tax rates that differ from the federal levels. It is important to understand the specific rules and thresholds in your state of residence.

Planning for Multiple States: If you own property in multiple states, consider the estate tax implications in each location and plan accordingly to minimize potential liabilities.

Strategies for Reducing Estate Taxes

Utilizing the Lifetime Exemption

Gift and Estate Tax Unified Exemption: The federal estate and gift tax exemptions are unified, allowing you to transfer assets up to the exemption amount during your lifetime or at death without incurring taxes. Strategically using this exemption can reduce the size of your taxable estate.

Annual Gift Exclusion: Take advantage of the annual gift exclusion, which allows you to gift up to $17,000 per recipient in 2024 without affecting your lifetime exemption. Regular gifting can effectively reduce your estate's value over time.

Establishing Trusts

Irrevocable Life Insurance Trust (ILIT): An ILIT holds life insurance policies outside of your taxable estate, ensuring that the death benefit is not subject to estate taxes. This strategy preserves the full value of the insurance payout for your beneficiaries.

Grantor Retained Annuity Trust (GRAT): A GRAT allows you to transfer asset appreciation to beneficiaries with minimal gift tax implications. You retain an annuity for a specified term, and any remaining assets pass to beneficiaries tax-free.

Charitable Remainder Trust (CRT): A CRT provides income to you or other beneficiaries for a set period, with the remainder going to a designated charity. This strategy offers an income tax deduction and reduces the taxable estate.

Leveraging Portability

Spousal Portability: Portability allows a surviving spouse to use any unused portion of their deceased spouse's federal estate tax exemption. This effectively doubles the exemption amount available to married couples, reducing potential estate taxes.

Timely Elections: Ensure that the portability election is made on the deceased spouse's estate tax return, filed within nine months of their death (with a possible six-month extension).

Family Limited Partnerships (FLPs)

Transferring Interests: FLPs allow you to transfer business interests to family members at a discounted value, reducing the taxable estate. This strategy also provides control over the business while transferring ownership.

Valuation Discounts: FLPs can apply valuation discounts for lack of marketability and minority interest, further reducing the estate's value for tax purposes.

Charitable Giving

Charitable Contributions: Charitable donations reduce the taxable estate and provide income tax deductions. Consider including charitable giving as part of your estate plan to support causes you care about while achieving tax benefits.

Donor-Advised Funds: Establish a donor-advised fund to make charitable contributions over time. This approach offers flexibility and immediate tax benefits while allowing you to direct donations to specific charities.

Maximizing the Step-Up in Basis

Capital Gains Tax Reduction: When assets are inherited, their cost basis is typically "stepped up" to their fair market value at the time of the owner's death. This step-up minimizes capital gains taxes if the assets are sold.

Strategic Asset Selection: Consider which assets will benefit most from a step-up in basis, and plan accordingly to optimize tax efficiency for your beneficiaries.

Considerations for Effective Tax Planning

Regularly Review and Update Your Plan

Changing Laws and Circumstances: Estate and tax laws are subject to change, and personal circumstances may evolve over time. Regularly review and update your estate plan to ensure it remains aligned with current laws and your goals.

Professional Guidance: Work with experienced legal and financial advisors to navigate the complexities of estate tax planning and ensure that your strategies are effective and compliant.

Communicate with Family Members

Transparency and Understanding: Discuss your estate planning strategies with family members to ensure they understand your intentions and the rationale behind your decisions.

Preparing Successors: Prepare beneficiaries and successors for their roles and responsibilities in managing the estate and understanding the tax implications involved.

Plan for Liquidity Needs

Meeting Tax Obligations: Ensure that your estate has sufficient liquidity to meet tax obligations without forcing the sale of assets. Consider life insurance or other funding mechanisms to provide the necessary cash flow.

Business Succession Planning: If your estate includes a family business, plan for its continuity and address any liquidity challenges associated with transferring ownership.

By implementing these strategies and considerations, you can effectively navigate estate taxes and minimize their impact on your estate. Proactive tax planning preserves more wealth for your beneficiaries and ensures that your estate plan aligns with your financial goals and legacy.

12.2 Leveraging Trusts for Asset Protection and Tax Efficiency

Trusts are versatile estate planning tools that offer a range of benefits, including asset protection and tax efficiency. By strategically incorporating trusts into your estate plan, you can safeguard your assets from creditors, reduce tax liabilities, and ensure that your wealth is distributed according to your wishes. This section explores how trusts can be used to achieve these objectives.

Types of Trusts for Asset Protection

Irrevocable Trusts

Asset Separation: Irrevocable trusts are powerful tools for asset protection because assets transferred to these trusts are no longer considered part of your estate. This separation shields them from creditors and legal claims, provided the transfer is made before any claims arise.

Beneficiary Designations: You can specify beneficiaries and control the timing and conditions of distributions, ensuring that assets are used according to your wishes.

Tax Implications: Transferring assets to an irrevocable trust may have gift tax implications, but it also reduces the taxable estate, potentially lowering estate taxes.

Domestic Asset Protection Trusts (DAPTs)

Creditor Protection: DAPTs are designed specifically for asset protection, allowing you to retain some control over the trust assets while shielding them from creditors.

State-Specific Laws: DAPTs are available in certain states with favourable asset protection laws. These trusts require careful planning to ensure compliance with state regulations.

Spendthrift Trusts

Beneficiary Protection: Spendthrift trusts protect beneficiaries from creditors and their own financial mismanagement by restricting their access to the trust assets. The trustee retains control over distributions, providing an additional layer of protection.

Controlled Distributions: This type of trust is particularly useful for beneficiaries who may lack financial discipline or be vulnerable to external financial pressures.

Qualified Personal Residence Trusts (QPRTs)

Home Protection: A QPRT allows you to transfer your primary or secondary residence into a trust while retaining the right to live there for a specified term. This reduces the value of your taxable estate and provides asset protection for your home.

Future Transfer: After the term ends, the property is transferred to the beneficiaries, often at a reduced tax value, minimizing gift and estate taxes.

Trusts for Tax Efficiency

Grantor Retained Annuity Trusts (GRATs)

Transfer Appreciation: GRATs are used to transfer the appreciation of an asset to beneficiaries with minimal gift tax consequences. The grantor receives an annuity for a specified term, and any remaining assets pass to the beneficiaries tax-free.

Low-Interest Environments: GRATs are particularly effective in low-interest-rate environments, allowing more appreciation to be transferred tax-free.

Charitable Remainder Trusts (CRTs)

Income and Tax Benefits: CRTs provide a stream of income to you or other beneficiaries for a set period, with the remainder going to a designated charity. This strategy offers an immediate income tax deduction and reduces estate taxes.

Capital Gains Tax Avoidance: Transferring appreciated assets to a CRT allows them to be sold without incurring capital gains taxes, maximizing the value of the gift.

Charitable Lead Trusts (CLTs)

Charitable Giving and Tax Benefits: A CLT provides income to a charity for a set period, after which the remaining assets are transferred to your heirs. This reduces estate and gift taxes while supporting charitable causes.

Strategic Philanthropy: CLTs are useful for individuals who wish to support charities while minimizing transfer taxes on their estate.

Intentionally Defective Grantor Trusts (IDGTs)

Income Tax Benefits: An IDGT allows the grantor to pay income taxes on the trust's income, effectively reducing the estate's value while allowing the trust assets to grow tax-free for the beneficiaries.

Sale of Appreciated Assets: You can sell appreciated assets to an IDGT without triggering capital gains taxes, further enhancing tax efficiency.

Strategies for Effective Trust Planning

Tailored Solutions: Work with legal and financial advisors to create trust structures that align with your specific goals and circumstances. Customized trusts provide flexibility and control over asset management and distribution.

Multi-Trust Strategy: Consider using a combination of trusts to address different aspects of your estate plan, such as asset protection, tax efficiency, and charitable giving.

Regular Reviews and Updates

Changing Laws and Circumstances: Regularly review and update your trusts to ensure they comply with current laws and reflect changes in your financial situation or family dynamics.

Adapting to Change: Be open to modifying trust terms and structures as needed to adapt to new circumstances or opportunities.

Collaborate with Professionals

Legal and Financial Expertise: Collaborate with experienced legal and financial advisors to navigate the complexities of trust planning. Advisors can provide valuable insights and help implement effective strategies.

Comprehensive Planning: Ensure that your trust planning is integrated with your overall estate plan, addressing all aspects of asset management, tax efficiency, and wealth transfer.

Clear Communication with Beneficiaries

Transparent Intentions: Communicate your intentions and the purpose of each trust to your beneficiaries, ensuring they understand the reasoning behind your decisions.

Setting Expectations: Clearly outline the roles and responsibilities of trustees and beneficiaries to prevent misunderstandings and foster collaboration.

By leveraging trusts for asset protection and tax efficiency, you can create a robust estate plan that preserves your wealth, minimizes tax liabilities, and ensures that your assets are distributed according to your wishes. Thoughtful trust planning provides peace of mind and secures your legacy for future generations.

12.3 The Role of Life Insurance in Estate Planning

Life insurance is a critical component of a comprehensive estate plan, offering financial security, liquidity, and tax advantages. It can be used to provide for loved ones, cover estate taxes, and ensure the smooth transfer of wealth. Understanding how to effectively incorporate life insurance into your estate plan can enhance your strategy, protect your family, and help achieve your long-term goals. This section explores the role of life insurance in estate planning and provides guidance on how to leverage its benefits.

Key Benefits of Life Insurance in Estate Planning

Providing Financial Security for Beneficiaries

Income Replacement: Life insurance can replace lost income, ensuring that your dependents maintain their standard of living after your death. This is especially important for young families or households that rely on a single income.

Educational Funding: Proceeds from a life insurance policy can be earmarked for specific purposes, such as funding a child's education or paying off a mortgage. This provides peace of mind knowing that your financial responsibilities will be met.

Covering Estate Taxes and Debts

Estate Tax Liquidity: For large estates, life insurance can provide the liquidity needed to pay estate taxes without forcing the sale of assets. This is particularly valuable for estates that include illiquid assets, such as real estate or closely held businesses.

Debt Settlement: Life insurance can be used to settle outstanding debts, ensuring that your beneficiaries receive their inheritance free of encumbrances. This helps protect your estate from being depleted by creditors.

Equalizing Inheritance

Balancing Distributions: If you wish to leave specific assets, such as a family business, to one heir, life insurance can be used to provide equivalent value to other heirs. This strategy helps prevent disputes and ensures a fair distribution of your estate.

Addressing Unique Needs: Life insurance can also be used to provide for beneficiaries with special needs, ensuring they receive ongoing support without jeopardizing their eligibility for government benefits.

Funding Buy-Sell Agreements

Business Succession Planning: In family-owned businesses, life insurance is often used to fund buy-sell agreements. This ensures that the business can be transferred smoothly to the next generation or surviving partners, without financial strain.

Ensuring Continuity: The death benefit from a life insurance policy can be used to buy out the deceased owner's share, providing liquidity and preventing the forced sale of the business.

Types of Life Insurance Policies

Term Life Insurance

Coverage for a Specific Period: Term life insurance provides coverage for a specified period, such as 10, 20, or 30 years. It is often more affordable than permanent life insurance, making it an attractive option for those needing coverage during key life stages.

Pure Protection: Term policies are designed to provide a death benefit without any cash value accumulation. They are ideal for covering temporary needs, such as income replacement or mortgage protection.

Whole Life Insurance

Lifetime Coverage: Whole life insurance provides coverage for the insured's entire life, with a guaranteed death benefit. It also includes a cash value component that grows over time, offering a savings element.

Cash Value Benefits: The cash value can be accessed during the insured's lifetime through loans or withdrawals, providing additional financial flexibility. This can be useful for covering unexpected expenses or supplementing retirement income.

Universal Life Insurance

Flexible Premiums and Death Benefits: Universal life insurance offers flexibility in premium payments and the ability to adjust the death benefit. This allows policyholders to tailor the coverage to their changing needs and financial situation.

Cash Value Accumulation: Like whole life, universal life policies accumulate cash value that can be accessed during the insured's lifetime. The cash value earns interest based on market conditions or a guaranteed minimum rate.

Survivorship Life Insurance

Coverage for Multiple Lives: Survivorship life insurance, also known as second-to-die insurance, covers two lives (typically spouses) and pays out the death benefit after the second insured person dies. This type of policy is often used in estate planning to provide liquidity for estate taxes.

Estate Preservation: Survivorship policies are particularly useful for preserving wealth in large estates, as they provide funds to cover estate taxes or other liabilities, allowing heirs to inherit assets intact.

Strategies for Incorporating Life Insurance into Your Estate Plan

Establishing an Irrevocable Life Insurance Trust (ILIT)

Removing Insurance from Taxable Estate: An ILIT is a trust designed to own life insurance policies, removing the death benefit from the insured's taxable estate. This strategy reduces estate taxes and ensures that the full value of the insurance proceeds benefits your heirs.

Controlled Distributions: The trustee of the ILIT manages the policy and distributes the proceeds according to your instructions, providing control over how and when beneficiaries receive their inheritance.

Avoiding Estate Taxes: By placing the policy in an ILIT, you can avoid estate taxes on the life insurance proceeds, potentially saving your estate a significant amount of money.

Using Life Insurance for Charitable Giving

Charitable Remainder Trust (CRT) Funding: Life insurance can be used to fund a charitable remainder trust, providing a stream of income for beneficiaries and leaving the remainder to a charity. The death benefit from the policy can replace the value of the donated assets for your heirs.

Naming a Charity as Beneficiary: You can designate a charity as the beneficiary of a life insurance policy, providing a significant gift while potentially receiving an income tax deduction.

Life Insurance for Estate Equalization

Ensuring Fairness: If you have multiple heirs and want to leave a specific asset, such as a business or property, to one of them, life insurance can provide equal value to the other heirs. This approach prevents disputes and ensures a fair distribution of your estate.

Customizing Inheritances: Life insurance allows you to customize inheritances based on the unique needs and circumstances of each beneficiary, providing flexibility and ensuring that your wishes are honoured.

Considerations for Selecting the Right Policy

Assessing Your Needs

Financial Obligations: Consider your current and future financial obligations, such as income replacement, debt repayment, and educational expenses, when determining the amount of coverage needed.

Long-Term Goals: Align your life insurance policy with your long-term estate planning goals, such as providing for dependents, covering estate taxes, or supporting charitable causes.

Evaluating Costs

Premium Affordability: Choose a policy that fits within your budget while providing adequate coverage. Term life insurance may be more affordable for short-term needs, while whole or universal life insurance offers long-term benefits.

Policy Features: Evaluate the features of different policies, such as cash value accumulation, premium flexibility, and death benefit guarantees, to determine which best meets your needs.

Consulting with Professionals

Financial and Estate Advisors: Work with financial and estate planning professionals to determine the most effective way to incorporate life insurance into your estate plan. They can help you select the right policy and structure it in a way that maximizes benefits and minimizes taxes.

Regular Policy Reviews: Periodically review your life insurance policy to ensure it continues to meet you

By strategically incorporating life insurance into your estate plan, you can provide financial security for your loved ones, ensure liquidity for estate expenses, and achieve your philanthropic goals. Life insurance offers flexibility and control, making it a valuable tool in preserving your legacy and ensuring that your wishes are carried out.

Conclusion

Estate planning is more than just a series of legal and financial steps; it is an opportunity to ensure that your life's work and values are preserved for future generations. By thoughtfully crafting an estate plan, you can provide for your loved ones, protect your assets, minimize tax burdens, and create a legacy that reflects your personal beliefs and aspirations.

Throughout this book, we've explored the various elements of estate planning, from understanding the importance of wills and trusts to navigating complex family dynamics, planning for digital assets, and leveraging life insurance. Each component plays a crucial role in building a comprehensive estate plan tailored to your unique circumstances.

The process of estate planning requires careful consideration of both the present and the future. It involves making decisions that align with your values while also addressing the practical needs of your beneficiaries. Whether you are planning for a young family, ensuring the continuity of a family business, or preserving wealth for future generations, the strategies discussed in this book provide a foundation for making informed decisions.

It is important to remember that estate planning is not a one-time task but an ongoing process. Life changes—such as the birth of a child, a change in marital status, or a shift in financial circumstances—may necessitate updates to your plan. Regular reviews and consultations with experienced legal and financial advisors will ensure that your estate plan remains effective and aligned with your goals.

As you move forward with your estate planning journey, keep in mind the core principles of communication, flexibility, and foresight. Open dialogue with your family members, a willingness to adapt to changing circumstances, and a clear vision of your legacy will help you create an estate plan that not only meets your current needs but also honours your long-term intentions.

In conclusion, estate planning is an essential part of securing your legacy and providing for those you care about. By taking the time to thoughtfully plan, you can achieve peace of mind knowing that your assets are protected, your wishes will be carried out, and your loved ones will be supported in the years to come. Your legacy reflects your life's work, and through careful estate planning, you can ensure that it endures, making a positive impact on the lives of others long after you are gone.

www.ingramcontent.com/pod-product-compliance
Lightning Source LLC
Chambersburg PA
CBHW061313220326
41599CB00026B/4859